SPEAKING SECRETS for the **BORED ROOM**

REGINAL SMITH

Speaking Secrets for the Bored Room
copyright 2004 by Reginal Smith
All rights reserved

CONTENTS

Dedication

I dedicate this book to the one person who has always stood at my side. You would not be reading this book if it was not for the love and support of my best friend, my wife, Marilyn L. Smith. Also, I would like to thank Dave Butcher for his unfailing support and advice. A special thanks to my support teams at Dunn + Associates and Susan Kendrick's.

Acknowledgements

A good book cannot be written in isolation. Every book is a collaborative effort of many individuals who sometimes remain in the shadows. I want to take this time to thank those individuals who help to make this book possible. This book would not be what it is without their steady hands. I want to thank Graham Van Dixhorn for his hard work on making my words more palatable for you the reader. I want to thank Kathi Dunn for the fantastic front cover design. I would also like to thank Lee Lewis who did the interior design. All these individuals took a good book and made it a better book.

INTRODUCTION

If you are reading this book and you're only interested in learning to speak in front of a group, then return my book to the store and get your money back immediately. This book is not just about learning how to speak. This book is designed to change your life and the lives of those with whom you communicate. This is not a learning manual: It is a transformational vehicle. I wrote this book because learning to speak in public has transformed the lives of hundreds of individuals who have gone through my public speaking seminar. They've become successful leaders who have gone on to impact the lives of thousands of people.

All leaders need to know how to communicate well with others. And I have a shocker for you. You are a leader. Whenever you speak to a group of people, you assume the role of a leader. Everyone takes on a leadership role at one time or another. Whether it's in the home, community, at work, or in your family, leadership is simply the ability to get things done. To get things done today, you must know how to get others to work with you. And in order to be successful, you have to be able to articulate your ideas to others. Nothing is more powerful than to have other people latch on to your ideas. That's what made Bill Gates the richest man in the world in just a few short years: leadership.

Public speaking is a powerful tool with far-reaching consequences for every aspect of your life. It builds confidence in yourself and your ideas. It lets people know who you are, and what you value. It can help you get promoted, or get grant money, or get started in your own business, or even improve your relationships with others. We live in an information world. Information is the key to success and wealth. Why would you allow a public speaking impediment to handicap you from achieving your goals? As a good public speaker you will be admired, adored, and respected. It will open entirely new avenues for you.

When polls are taken of the general public, speaking in public consistently ranks among the top five fears that people have. It is up there with divorce, death, and moving to a new location. Why do so many people have a fear of speaking in public? The fear of public speaking is generated by the fear of the unknown. We fear that which we do not understand. Since most people do not receive training in public speaking, most of us fear it and do not do it very well.

For others they are able to cobble together a few ideas and speak, but the majority of people who are presenting information to the public do not do a very good job of it. And we the public accept the mediocrity because we don't know any better. We don't demand that those who speak before us are adequately prepared to deliver the information. I can remember when my eyesight started going bad. I would squint at restaurant menus and blink my eyes to see street signs at night. Finally, I went to an eye doctor who fitted me with a pair of glasses. Suddenly, the world looked different. Everything was so clear, and the colors so vibrant and alive. Street signs looked like works of art. Now that I can see, I will never go back to not wearing glasses. It is the same when it comes to public speaking. Our ears have been dulled by the monotony of bad speakers to the point where we think that the whole world is fuzzy and dull. But every now and then, we get a glimpse of what a really good speaker can do.

Why did I write this book? I am a busy entrepreneur with several business concerns, and taking the time to write can be difficult for me. I much prefer speaking in front of an audience, or teaching my public speaking seminar course first hand, to writing a book. Yet I recognize that a book is a great medium for meeting you first hand. I want to reach out to more people with the same transformational knowledge and skills I've shared over the years with hundred of managers, directors, employees, and students in my classrooms. I want to share with you my *love* of public speaking, and show what an incredible difference it has made in my own life and in the lives of others. We are not the same people we once were.

My larger goal is to reach enough of an audience that the general competence of public speaking—what you and I listen to everyday—begins to improve. With this book I am throwing down the gauntlet to speakers everywhere to work at their craft. To you the non-professional speaker, I hope you take up the challenge to learn to speak like the pros.

My purpose is to help you become a confident, effective speaker, to make you stand out above the crowd. I'll do this by sharing my 20 years experience of teaching public speaking in a classroom setting. Now, I am warning you: There is no book on the market today that will make you a great public speaker. That's sort of like reading a book to become a great surgeon. A surgeon has to study and then learns the trade through interactions with others and through practice. It's the same when it comes to learning how to be a brilliant speaker. You need to get out there and speak and receive feedback on your performance. No book can provide that sort of experience.

But what this book does, which makes it unique from all the other books on the market, is get to the essentials of what makes a great speech. I could have devoted thousands of pages of ink to all things needed to make you a great speaker. But I have extracted what I consider the best techniques and put them into this book. Some things I left out because I believe they add as much value by their absence as by their inclusion. I am more interested in the *quality*, and not the quantity, of the ideas. It is better for you to concentrate your energies in areas that will provide the most payback with the minimum investment of time.

Speaking of time, you will need to take some time to pour over this book. There are a few exercises in the book that will help you incorporate what you learn into your speaking. I designed the exercises to be relevant to everyday thinking and acting. The power of great speaking is to make all the hard work look easy. It's like being with a master chef. It all looks so simple and quick. Yet you are seeing the culmination of years of experience, know-how, and love in just a few short minutes. Your public speaking should look just the same and have the same feeling. You sweat during the preparation, and then appear to effortlessly deliver your message.

How to Use this Book

There are two great advances that define our modern era. The first is Newton's discovery of gravity and the second is Einstein's Theory of Relativity. The world hasn't been the same since these once-radical ideas became accepted scientific facts. But did Newton *discover* gravity or Einstein relativity? Well, of course not: The forces these great men identified have always been with us. But the scientific theories they created give us a framework and a new vocabulary to understand our universe and our place within it. These theories give us a sense of order, with rules and principles to guide us.

In this book I lay out the **Theory of Giving a Great Presentation**. This theory proves that good presentations are ordered, derived from rules and principles that we all will do well to follow. By following these rules and principles you will never freeze up, or be unprepared, or bore your audience again. What's even more exciting is that the principles you're about to learn are applicable whenever you're called on to express yourself in public.

The Theory of Giving a Great Presentation states that all effective presentations should be informative, have an impact on the audience, and never be boring. To achieve this, I have created the *Effective Presentation Pyramid*. The pyramid is divided into five levels. Each level represents an essential principle in the theory. Each level is interrelated to all the levels that follow. The final step, the delivery, is what I consider the apex, or the final goal, of a great speech. All the other levels will lead you to the final level of mastery. Each chapter in the book will explain each level in the pyramid. In order to have the greatest impact on making an effective delivery, I suggest you follow through the levels as you create your speech.

The pyramid provides a structure upon which to construct a powerful speech. I have stripped all the elements of speaking down to the essentials. I do not wish to load you down with a lot of extraneous information. I do not want you to have too much to think about. The levels are designed to get you started developing and giving your speech as soon as possible.

The Theory of Giving a Great Presentation consists of five levels. Each provides the foundation to support the next level. The levels are as follows:

Level I - Information/Outlining is the foundation of every good speech. Information has to be gathered, analyzed, and organized.

Level II - A Message has to be crafted for every speech. Speeches are message driven and the message is driven by a goal.

Level III - A Structure organizes the speech into a logical format.

Level IV - Proper **Preparation** ensures you are ready for every contingency.

Level V - The Delivery should be dynamic, informative, and have an impact on the audience. It should move your listeners to take action.

LEVEL V
DELIVERY

LEVEL IV PREPARATION

LEVEL III STRUCTURE

LEVEL II MESSAGE

LEVEL I INFORMATION/OUTLINING

The Effective Presentation Pyramid

In order to facilitate immediate results, in the first sections of the book I leave the icing off and just give you the cake. The icing consists of **Power Techniques** that I have included as a separate section of the book. These are six high-end speaking techniques that will transform your presentation from a good one to a great one. These techniques will help keep your audience riveted and entertained.

Also included is a set of rules of the universe that I call **Reggie's Rules**. These are rules that I have created out of the hard knocks of the speaking business. I did not want to put them in one place, because they can be misunderstood if they are not viewed in context. So I have placed Reggie's Rules in strategic locations where they will make the most sense. Look for Reggie's Rules. By the way, if you feel there are some additional rules that you think other readers will find helpful, drop me a line.

I added a few definitions to the book. These are terms I have created—or borrowed—to form the distinctive vocabulary of my Presentation Theory.

I have also included some helpful exercises. I designed them to be short, quick, and easy. They're here to help you put into practice everything you're learning. Make sure you do the exercises. They will help you to increase your speaking effectiveness.

I hope these conventions will help you get the maximum benefit from your investment of time and effort. If you follow my program and apply the rules and techniques you find here I guarantee you will be more effective in your presentations—and feel a great sense of accomplishment. So don't delay: Get started right now!

LEVEL I

INFORMATION/OUTLINING

"Where shall I begin, please your Majesty?" I asked.
"Begin at the beginning," the King said gravely,
"and go on till you come to the end: then stop."

Lewis Carroll, Alice's Adventures In Wonderland, *(1865)*

Information is the foundation upon which great speeches are built. In this step you will learn how to lay a solid foundation. If the information in your speech is not solid and firmly constructed, the entire speech may collapse. It is important to get the information correct from the start.

Information is more than just cold facts. Information can inspire, teach, and give your listeners something to think about. How do you get information? How do you prepare your information?

This is the smallest step in the book, but it contains some powerful gems to help you in your information-gathering phase. If you get this right, it will set the tone for the rest of your presentation. There are three steps in Level I. The steps are:

1) Identify your topic
2) Research your topic
3) Outline your topic

1. Identify Your Topic

It may seem obvious, but it's nice to know what you are going to be speaking about. For the majority of your speaking opportunities you will not choose the topic. At times you might need to make a presentation—and I personally find such situations to be more exciting—on a subject that is totally unknown to you. But extemporaneous, "off the top of your head" speeches are rare: Usually you know in advance what the topic is going to be and have some familiarity with it. Whatever your topic, identify it up front and make sure you and your audience are on the same page.

Once I delivered a great speech before a very enthusiastic crowd. They loved it and thanked me, but on my way out someone pointed out that I had not spoken on the subject they had been expecting. Fortunately, no one else seemed to recognize the error.

2. Research Your Topic

This is the fun part of gathering your information. You have different paths to choose from here. Each will yield a wealth of rewards for your presentation. Here are some questions to help you in your research.

What if you are already familiar with the subject? Familiarity helps, but you still need to do research on your topic. Researching the topic anew can add fresh anecdotes, statistics, and insights to your presentation. You need to find out if your knowledge is on par with what the industry or the leading experts are saying. In today's information world, no one person knows it all. Many experts today are very narrowly focused in a particular sub-area of a topic, with less knowledge about other aspects of the same topic. You need to make sure that your knowledge of your topic is not built upon misinformation or out-of-date facts. Ensure that you can answer any question and back up your facts during your presentation.

What if you are not familiar with the topic? If you are speaking on a subject you know little about, you need to ensure that you do due diligence in your research. Many of the same points mentioned above will apply. In addition, since you are not an expert in the topic, you need to acquire an education about the topic so that you can appear to be an expert to your audience. You don't have to know everything about the topic, but you should know more than the casual observer. This may require a great deal of research on your part.

How should you research the topic? Look for sources of information. Today, those sources are readily available to us in a variety of media. The public libraries are prime sources of help today as in days past. All librarians are information savvy, and ready to help research any topic. For me, the library is still the best researching tool available to us today. Librarians are the unsung heroes of our society. If you work for a large firm, the *corporate* library can be a rich source of material for your topic.

What about the Internet? It is a great place to *look* for information. But let the consumer beware: Not everything that glitters is gold. On the Internet it may not be possible to verify that the information you want to use is accurate or up to date. Make sure your research verifies the accuracy and suitability of the information. If you are taking information from a website, make sure that it is a reputable site. Information that is pulled down from the web should be verified with information from other sources. With such caution in mind, however, the web can be a great place to retrieve information quickly.

What kind of information works best in an oral presentation? There are four primary sources of data that work well for verbal presentations. I have listed them in the order of what has the most impact:

- **Statistics**—Hard numbers are always good to have. Numbers can be put into a visual format.
- **Case Studies**—People like to know if someone else has used a product, service, or concept. How did this benefit the person or the organization?
- **Testimony**—Give quotes from experts in the field. Make sure that the person you are quoting is well known and reputable.
- **Definitions**—Technical terms and definitions can be very useful in explaining a complicated subject. If your listeners are not familiar with the terms, be prepared to explain them and to offer clear, well-worded definitions.

THREE KEYS TO COLLECTING DATA

1. Accurate

2. Up to date

3. Relevant to the topic

There is one source of information that is often overlooked, and when it is used it is often mishandled. What source is that? *Humans.* Yes, our fellow humans are a wealth of facts, stories, and wisdom. Even if you have a certain amount of expertise on a topic, it is always good to hear what other "experts" have to say on the subject. People can enhance your understanding of a subject, and may even direct you to other sources of information. In order to enlist someone's help, you should perform an interview. An interview is simply organized gathering of information from someone who has expertise in the topic you are researching.

EXERCISE #1

How to conduct an interview

The first step: **Identify the people** you think can be the most help. Write down all the names of individuals who may have knowledge that will help you with your subject. Write down as many names as you can. When you are done, select the individuals you think will be able to give you the most information and help. Unless the subject is very complex, interviewing 2-3 people should be sufficient to get you on the right track.

Second step: **Set up the interview.** Call the person on the phone. Don't email: It's too impersonal. Tell her what you are doing and that you would like to interview her. The majority of people will say "yes". That's because we all like nothing better than to talk about ourselves and what we know. While it's preferable to do your interviews in person, busy people may prefer a phone interview. Either way, set a time and keep your appointment.

Third Step: **Prepare your questions**. Write out the questions you are going to ask. Should you send the questions in advance? Maybe. But sometimes it's helpful to get initial reactions to questions to get a sense of where your interviewee is coming from. Use your best judgment and act accordingly. All questions should be direct, with a view toward helping you understand your topic better.

Fourth Step: **The interview**. Arrive on time. Being late is a sign of disrespect. Take along a note pad and pen. Take brief notes.

Fifth Step: **Send a thank you letter.** Email or send a thank you note. A hand written note is the best way to thank a person. It's more personal.

At this stage you are not making any decisions as to what information is relevant or not. Gather your information regardless of what you may be thinking at the moment.

3. Outline Your Topic

Now we move on to assessing the information for its value and giving it some basic organization. With the topic in mind, start looking at the information you have collected. You will only be presenting a part of all the information you have collected. But what information should you put into your speech? Look for information that supports the particular points that you wish to make in the presentation. As you review the information, start writing down the main points that come to mind. What are your notes telling you about this subject? Get your ideas organized into an outline. I am going to discuss five well-used outlines.

Topical. Many speakers organize their ideas in a topical outline. In a topical outline, you write out the topic of your speech at the top of the page. Then underneath the topic, you lay out the main points of your topic. Each main point will have a series of sub points that support your main point. You can use numbers or letters to separate out the points. The main heading ideas will give you some areas where you can place the information you have gathered. Here's a sample of a topical outline.

Subject: Budget for Sub Prime Project

1. Cost of equipment
   a. Computers
   b. Telephones

2. Cost of software
3. Cost of employees
   a. Consultants
   b. Full time employees

Under each of these subheadings, enter information to support or explain the subheading area. These outline areas become pockets in which to place your information. Of course, as you are analyzing the material you may come up with more headings for the information you have gathered. At this point it does not matter how many headings you have. Just go ahead and organize them. This will give you a good place to put all the information in plain view for your examination.

Process Outline. In this type of outline, you lay out the steps you want your listeners to understand. You are laying out a process and explaining how all these steps fit together to give a final result. Here's an example of a process outline. If the topic you have chosen is How to Buy a Car, you can write an outline of the steps to buying a car. For example:

Purchase a Car
      A. Research car
      B. Find right dealership
      C. Negotiate purchase

Problem/Solution Outline. This is a fairly common outline which lends itself to audiences accepting a solution you are proposing. In the beginning of the outline you state the problem. Once the problem is stated, you develop your points around how to solve the problem. This can lead to some very interesting twists. In the outline you could lay out some alternate solutions that don't work, then detail the shortcomings of the alternates, then lay out the solution you were proposing all along. This can be very powerful, because it gives your audience different solutions—some they may have considered and some they may not have—and shows how each one plays out.

Proof Statement. In this way of organizing your material you start off with a statement of fact. Then you use the rest of the outline to support the particular statement you make.

Sentence Outline. This is a simple method. Here you write out a series of sentences expressing your ideas. The sentences should be short and address one point per sentence.

As you can see, there are lots of ways you can lay out and organize material, but I believe the topical outline will serve you best in preparing for most of your presentations. Do what works for you. You can even mix and match them as you see fit.

With your outline completed, start making notations under each point for ideas you think will support each point. What information will support each idea? When looking at supporting data, use information that supports the particular point you wish to make to your audience. Remember: Your audience is the key. During this whole process it is important for you to always keep your listener in mind. What do they need to know? What vital information will benefit them? Always keep the needs of the listener in front of you.

Now with your outline prepared, it's time to trim the trees. There's a good chance that you have either too much information, or that you have some facts that do not lend strong support to your main headings. Maybe you're trying to cover too many main points. So how do you trim the trees?

I once saw a movie in which a young man was being taught how to trim a Bonsai tree. It was his first time trimming a Bonsai tree, and he was nervous that he would do a bad job and damage the tree. When he asked for instructions from his teacher, the teacher replied, "Cut away everything that is not a tree." The same advice applies to preparing your presentation. Look back over your material and cut away everything that does not directly support your main point. Oh, yes, I am sure you have some interesting side facts, but if they don't lend support to what you are saying, trim them away.

I recommend that if you are using a topical outline, do not use more than five main points, and if possible limit them to three. Most people will not be able to absorb more than three main points.

This is where you can practice consolidation. Perhaps there are some main points that can be folded into other main points. Keep working at this until you feel you have broken your speech down into its most basic elements.

Great! Your presentation is ready. By the way, don't throw away any of the information you've trimmed off your speech. It may come in handy later on in the process. Now, with your outline in hand, you're ready to move on to the next level.

LESSONS LEARNED

Information/Outlining

- Identify Your Topic
- Research Your Topic
- Outline Your Idea

Five Outlines

- Topical - Main points arranged in a logical order.
- Process - Material laid out in logical steps to follow.
- Problem/Solution - Problem is stated. Solution is offered.
- Proof Statement - State a fact. Provide supporting information.
- Sentence Outline - Use short sentences to lay out main ideas.

LEVEL II
DEVELOPING YOUR MESSAGE

"He is one of those orators of whom it is said, 'Before they get up, they do not know what they are going to say; when they are speaking, they do not know what they are saying; and when they have sat down, they do not know what they had said.'"

Winston Churchill, Speech in the British House of Commons, 1906

Based on your work in Level I, the information is now organized for your topic. You've got your sub points and supporting material to flesh out and support the main points. The next step is to build a bridge to your audience by "packaging" your information. You package your information by developing your message. Every speech should be message driven. In this step we will learn how to create a compelling message.

Developing your message is a critical step in making a great speech. The message is the *theme* of your presentation. It should wind through your speech like threads in fabric. The message is the central idea and focus of your presentation. The message is what you are seeking to impart to the minds of your listeners. It is the mental takeaway from your presentation.

Developing a clear message might seem like a simple step. Yet this is the most overlooked step in the entire speaking process, something of an afterthought. Most speakers are so wrapped up in writing and delivering the speech that they fail to consider how to formulate the message. May *that* never happen when it comes to your presentation! The message is the core reason for making your presentation. It is your responsibility to make your audience understand your message, loud and clear and without confusion.

Goal-Driven Messages

Before we can craft the message, we have to understand the goal. Every speech needs a goal. A goal is a desired action, what you want the audience to do with the information. The first step in crafting the message is to understand that the message is goal-driven. The goal sets the target you wish to reach.

To establish your goal, begin with the end of the speech. At the conclusion of your presentation you expect a response. The expected response is the goal you wish to achieve. The expected response should be clear in your mind. It is important to understand the response you wish to receive from the audience. After all, you would not leave the house to go on a trip if you did not know the destination. To present effectively, you have to know your goal. The following exercise will help you to define your goal.

EXERCISE #2

How to Define Your Goal

Here's a little exercise to help you determine your goal. Get out a blank sheet of paper.

1. Close your eyes and picture yourself making the closing statements of your speech. What is it that you want from your audience?
2. Write your answer on the paper.

I want you to repeat steps 1 and 2 for each of the following questions:

- How should they feel when you finish speaking?
- What kind of impact do you want to make in their lives?
- Are you asking them to take a certain action? What is the action you want them to take?
- Do you want to influence them to think about something in a different way? What is the new thought or idea you wish to implant into their minds?

Take your time to think about your answers. They represent a key aspect of defining your goal: what you expect from the audience.

Take a good look at what you've written. Underline the answers that appeal to you. If some of them sound the same, then combine them. Look for key words and phrases. Try to distill the goal into a single sentence that focuses on one or two main ideas generated by the exercise. That single sentence is your goal.

My students always ask, "Does every speech need a goal? What if you are just speaking to share information that you think people need to know?" The simple answer to the question is "yes". Even if you are just getting out information, you should still have a goal in mind. Are people causing trouble for the accounting office by forgetting to file their expense reports? If you have to formally address this issue, think of it as a presentation. Give some thought to how to present your information in a way that persuades and influences your fellow employees to take the desired corrective action.

In the old days such explanations were not necessary. People simply did what they were told to do and did not ask a lot of questions. Those days are long gone and today, people demonstrate a much more skeptical view of authority. Here's a news flash for you: No one is going to be persuaded by your title or educational achievements. Real influence flows from authenticity.

In the workplace our bosses exercise influence mostly through **authoritative power** (their official positions). Their positions grant them a certain privilege of power. **Authentic power** is defined as power to persuade and influence others within an organization, regardless of one's title or position. Those with authentic power cannot be identified on any organizational chart. Authentic power is derived in part from the demonstrated ability to apply critical thinking skills in the real world. Authenticity instantly flows from the person who can clearly communicate ideas. Authentic power gives you, the well-prepared and articulate speaker, a unique advantage. By developing and honing your message, you gain authenticity, allowing you to tap into the wellspring of human emotions to persuade and influence your audience to accomplish your goal.

Factoid: Authoritative power is limited and temporary privilege. The privilege is to tell people what do. This type of power can be granted or taken away. Authentic power is unlimited and permanent, and is within the grasp of everyone reading this book.

Can a speech have multiple goals? Yes, but be careful: You don't want to have too many goals. Multiple goals may cause you to drift away from your main points. I have a theory when it comes to trying to achieve multiple goals in a speech. The more goals you try to reach, the more likely it is that the goals will be misunderstood or forgotten.

If possible try to narrow your goal down to one or two desired outcomes. You might be able to combine multiple goals into a single goal. Remember, it is your job as a speaker to ensure that you deliver a clear and coherent message. You may muddle your message and confuse your audience if you try to accomplish too many goals. To help your audience retain as much information as possible, keep the goal simple. Try to narrow the goal to one sentence. The last thing you want in a speech is complexity. Anything more than one sentence may be too complex for you to express and for your audience to process and retain.

Here are a few points that will help you to narrow down your goal. The goal should be S-M-A-R-T.

The Smart Goal

S - Specific
M - Measurable
A - Articulate the goal
R - Reasonable. It is possible to achieve
T - Targeted. Narrowed to focused action(s).

Let's apply the S-M-A-R-T goal to our recycling presentation. It is our goal to have the audience recycle. Is this goal S-M-A-R-T? Let's run the test. Is the goal specific? Yes, it's one action. Can it be measured? Yes, it will be done or not done. Can it be articulated? Yes. Is it reasonable? Yes, it is within the listeners' ability to perform the task. Is it targeted? Yes, it is focused on the individual who can have the maximum impact on the goal.

Now that you have a goal, you can work on your message. Perhaps you are thinking that the message and the goal can be the same thing. No, your goal is to alter behavior, change minds, influence and persuade. Your message is the mechanism that will help to achieve your goal. It may seem the same, but actually they are very different. Your goal is to modify behavior, the message is the means to reach the goal. For instance, let's say that your goal is to get everyone in your community to recycle. You are trying to influence people to do the right thing when it comes to recycling. But your *message* is to illustrate the importance of recycling. Your message will show how recycling saves the environment and saves money. You must craft the message in a way that achieves the goal of altering the behavior. If you simply state that recycling is good, then you may or may not alter the behavior. You would be leaving the result of your speech up to chance. Instead, in the course of the speech, you want to convince your audience that recycling is good, it is important that we do our share to save the planet, and so forth. Do you see the difference?

Must a presentation have a message? The short answer: Yes! Otherwise, why bother to put it together? For example, a senior level executive in a Fortune 500 company started having monthly meetings that were open to all employees. His style at the meeting was, to say the least, boring. I have had a more exciting time examining the lint in my pockets. When I told students in my class about it, they argued that since the executive was just passing on information, what was wrong with being boring? My response was that the executive could have achieved the same results with an email or newsletter. If the goal was to pass on information, why bother to go through the time and effort of having a meeting and preparing a presentation? No doubt this particular medium was carefully chosen to build some rapport with the people who worked for him. The meetings had the opposite effect; the executive came off as somewhat aloof and distant. Instead of building rapport, he seemed to have alienated the people he was trying to cultivate.

The executive *was* sending out a message. Unfortunately, it was not the message he had intended. It was as if, while he was speaking, there was a subtext underneath him reading, "I am powerful, I am Mr. Boss, and I am boring." And while he no doubt meant well, a good speech coach would have pointed out that his speaking style was sending a message of distance and aloofness. The moral of this story is that you send out a message whenever you speak.

In essence, a speech is about gathering and organizing information and presenting it to your audience. The audience should easily grasp what you are trying to tell them. The audience should also understand clearly what action(s) you wish them to take. Take a cue from television advertisement. By the end of the 30-60 second commercial you know exactly what the advertiser wants you to do. His goal is to get you to buy something. The message may be that your life will be enhanced, improved, or made easier through the use of this product or service. It is your job to accomplish the same thing with your audience. Your message clearly conveys how their lives are made better by achieving your goal.

Can there be multiple messages? Yes, but I would recommend against transmitting too many messages to your audience. If you make too many points, then your audience may not be able to recall them. A good message should fit into what many people call the "elevator speech". The elevator speech is one you use when you get on the elevator with your boss and she asks your opinion about a matter. Of course, you have less than a minute to speak your mind. That means you have to zero in on the main point and forget about everything else. That's how the message should be revealed in your speech. It is the one thing you want to stick out in their minds, the one unforgettable element in the entire presentation.

Connecting with Your Audience: Emotions

When framing your message, think emotions. That's a strange concept for the buttoned up, corporate world. You mean we have to deal with feelings? Yes, emotions are the most important leverage that a speaker has with an audience. You want to appeal to the emotions of your audience. Emotions, or feelings, are deeply connected to what people think. By tapping into emotions, you as a speaker are tapping into the deep level thinking of your audience. You need to reach down into their consciousness. What are their experiences, hopes, and dreams? Does your message connect with your audience at that level? By tapping into that spring of emotions, you open them up to your message. Emotions are the key to being able to influence and persuade your audience.

In framing your message in the emotional realm, keep in mind the *behavior* you wish to influence. The message is designed to influence a change in behavior. Once I was trying to get my company to purchase a particular software package. I knew there would be opposition since we already had a similar product. But the existing product did not have all the capabilities of the product I was proposing. My *goal* was to persuade the group of managers to purchase the new product. My *message* was that we needed to purchase this software if we wanted to be taken seriously in the corporate world. To do so I appealed to their emotions—the fear of failure and looking second rate—to influence them to purchase the software.

I want to share with you one of the most important rules for defining your message. It is a rule that will help you to think about your message and its importance. I call it **Reggie's Rule #1: The Principle of Justification**. It's based on the fact that we buy on emotion and justify with logic. Whatever decision we make, there is always emotion involved. We cannot escape it, because as human beings we are hardwired for emotions. All of our decisions are based on emotions: How do we feel about it? We make decisions based on those feelings and then use our logic to justify and validate our feelings and decisions.

But how do you know what your audience is feeling, what they've experienced, and what their hopes and dreams are? I am not going to give you a complex psychological method for determining audience emotion. You need a tool you can use immediately. Besides, there are many books on the market that cover this subject in much more detail than I can here (please see my reference list to read more on the subject). In keeping with my goal of giving you *essential speaking secrets you can use now*, I have grouped all human emotions into what I consider the most basic pair. For the purpose of crafting your message, emotions are based on either love or fear.

Reggie's Rule #2: The Principle of Love and Fear says that people are persuaded and influenced through either **love** or **fear**. We take certain actions because we want them to benefit us (love), or because we wish to avoid a negative consequence (fear). Both love and fear are powerful motivators *and* powerful deterrents. Both emotions are at the root of most of our decisions.

You probably purchased the car you have because you fell in love with it. Maybe as a kid you always saw yourself driving this car. You purchased the vehicle in order to recapture that emotion. Another example is the recent surge of SUV purchases. People want to feel safe, and they buy SUVs because they think they are safer, yet statistics show the opposite. We are always trying to meet certain emotional needs when making a purchase.

As a speaker, your message needs to appeal to what your audience fears or loves.

Playing on fears might seem manipulative, but the results of even fear can be positive. You might persuade your boss to purchase a particular computer system because the competition may be using the same system. You are appealing to your boss's fear of losing a competitive advantage if the purchase is not made. Your goal is not to scare him. Your goal is to improve the competitiveness of your company. I have used this particular argument to great success on many occasions in the corporate world. Remember, the key is to take into account the emotions of the audience.

If you are squeamish from all this talk of emotions, I have a more logical explanation for you to consider. Look at it from the point of positive or negative reinforcement, or affirmation. You can appeal to the audience affirming the benefits they will receive when taking the course of action you are recommending. Or you can speak of negative consequences, of what might occur if your recommended course of action is not followed. Positive and negative affirmation achieves the identical purpose of connecting with the emotions of your listeners. Everyone wants to feel good about making a decision.

By now you should have a sense of what you want to say, so let's take a look at who you'll be speaking to. First, let's go back to the outline you constructed in the previous step.

Goal: Get everyone to recycle trash
Message: TBD (To be Determined)

Main Points
       I. Planet is being overrun with trash
       II. Recycling reduces trash and pollution
       III. Recycling is more economical

Notice what I did with our recycling speech. I put the goal on the top. We want the audience to recycle: that's the goal of the speech. Next, outline the points that support the idea of getting everyone to recycle their trash. A good message will emerge from this process. In this case, I want to convey the message that recycling is good for our environment. However, this may not remain the message. It may evolve and develop beyond that, but we have what I call a "straw man" outline. Now we need to take a closer look at the audience.

Connecting with Your Audience: Who Are They and What Do They Know?

I hope I've made it clear that the audience is the primary reason for developing your goals and crafting your message. At this point, it's safe to make some assumptions about the audience. Assumptions are good, because the assumption becomes something you can count on. For example, if you have been asked by your superiors to make a sales presentation to a client, you make an assumption that you are presenting the correct material (sales pitch) to the correct audience (qualified recipients to your idea). Don't waste your time trying to convince someone to purchase a racehorse when they need a racecar. You need to make sure you are speaking to the right audience with the right message. No amount of preparation and work will help you if you miss this point. Some might find your presentation somewhat interesting and amusing, but it is unlikely to alter anyone's behavior.

Let me give you a quick example. Let's say you are in the business of selling mutual funds to the general public. Your message will change depending on the audience. The message to an older, retired audience might stress the safety of mutual funds, how the investments can guarantee a good steady stream of income, and so on. The older group is more interested in security than growth. If you were presenting this material to those who have just graduated from college, your goal is the same, but the message will be different. With a younger group you want to stress the importance of saving for the future. You want to show that mutual fund money invested in more speculative markets over time will garner the younger person a more secure retirement in the future. The common goal of getting the client to purchase the product is emphasized, yet with a different twist to appeal to different needs.

In order to help you refine your message for your audience, I have put together some questions you need to ask. Jot down the answers to these questions:

Who's my audience? This is the most important question to ask. Is the audience made up of clients? Is it your superiors, peers, or subordinates? What is the background of this audience in relationship to your subject? What issues or concerns will they have with respect to this topic?

What do they know about me? For an audience—any audience—to be open to your message you must establish credibility, trust, and rapport. What does the audience know about you? Is it positive? Great! You have something to build upon. Use that positive energy to motivate the audience. Do they have negative images of you, perhaps some negativity involving not you yourself, but the organization you are representing? Then you will have to work hard to build up credibility. You have to understand that you are starting with a deficit and must work your way up the trust ladder. There are many ways to build up credibility, and it's often easier if the audience does not know you. We cover this in more detail in Level V under the subheading *Presence*.

What do they know about the subject? Does your audience know anything at all about your topic? This is important to know in part because it determines the depth of detail you cover with information and explanations. If the audience has a high level of expertise, then perhaps certain jargon and terminology will not have to be explained. But be careful. Once while attending a technical briefing, a technical presenter went through his whole presentation using certain terms and jargon unfamiliar to his audience. They were totally lost because he hadn't answered the question: What do they know about the subject? On the other hand, I have seen a technical presenter actually turn and ask the audience if it was okay to delve into some of the finer details. With audience acquiescence, the presenter was able to dive down into the minutiae without worry. But all along the way he checked to ensure that he had not lost his audience.

If the audience lacks a high degree of knowledge on the subject, it is your job to present the material so that it is easily understood. Try to take what I call the "40,000-foot view" of the material. When you look down from that altitude you see major features of the earth's surface: mountains, lakes, forests, farmland, roads, and towns. You can't make out any road signs or billboards, but it's not necessary. It's the same with presenting material your audience is not familiar with. You need to give them a coherent overview of the subject, a basic outline of the lay of the land. Usually it's not necessary to go into great detail. But you should be prepared to zoom down and discuss the road signs and billboards. This often surfaces later on in the presentation or during question and answer time.

Connecting with Your Audience: Benefits, Benefits, Benefits!

People are primarily interested in themselves, not in you. I didn't invent this concept; it's at the core of persuasion. This principle is so important in getting buy-in from people that I've made it **Reggie's Rule No. #3: WIIFT—What's In It For Them?** It's what

STEPS TO INCREASE YOUR WIIFT

1. Write out the clear single purpose of your speech

2. Write down the exact benefits the audience will receive

3. Insert WIIFT into every main point in your outline

4. Restate your WIIFT in the conclusion of the presentation

your audience wants to know RIGHT NOW, and you need to deliver a satisfactory answer. Answer this question with a specific and meaningful benefit, and you will get through to them. This question needs to be addressed from the very beginning and reinforced throughout the presentation.

Your message is a vehicle for delivering the benefits of the information you are presenting. The listeners will want to know how your information will benefit them. Remember **Reggie's Rule #1: The Principle of Justification**? People buy on emotion, justify with logic. There's no stronger emotion than the love we have for ourselves, self-love, or *narcissism*, is not just about selfish choices; it's also about self-preservation. It is tempered by showing respect and love for others. But even in the most altruistic person there is a grain of self-love. We could not survive without it.

It is your job as a speaker to tap into this self-love and use it to your advantage. Your message must show how your service, product, suggestion, or plan will benefit your audience. Now don't confuse benefiting their *organization* with what is going to benefit them on a personal level. Sometimes you can combine the two, by pointing out that when the organization benefits, they will benefit. Everyone wants to look good to his or her organization.

There is nothing unethical about using emotions to influence people. We do this in our subconscious mind every day of our lives. Whether it's with our children, spouse, boss, or the traffic cop who's about to write us a ticket, we are always trying to influence someone. It's a legitimate tool. But like any tool, it can be—and certainly has been—misused. I draw the line at persuading people to do things that will cause harm to come to themselves or others. But if you care about your audience, that won't happen. In short, when your listeners benefit, you benefit. And I can't think of a better measure of success for a presentation than whether or not you have helped others to succeed.

This is the motivation I have for teaching presentation skills and for writing this book. Nothing compares to the feeling I get from influencing people to transform their lives by transforming their speaking skills. It's a win-win situation. So make me feel good: Use these methods to help you achieve your goals!

LESSONS LEARNED

Define Your Message –

- All speeches must be message-driven
- All messages must be goal-driven
- Limit your speech to a specific, definable goal
- Goals should be SMART:
  - **S**pecific
  - **M**easurable
  - **A**rticulated
  - **R**easonable
  - **T**argeted

Understand Your Audience –

- Who's my audience?
- What do they know about me?
- What do they know about the subject?

Connect with the Audience –

- Remember . . . Benefits, benefits, benefits.

LEVEL III
STRUCTURE

"In architecture as in all other operative arts, the end must direct the operation. The end is to build well. Well building hath three conditions. Commodity, firmness, and delight."

Henry Wooten, Elements of Architecture, *1624*

When my wife and I had our first home built, it was a great experience. We chose the floor plan and the colors and the carpet. When they started to build the house, we went out to take a look at it. We were like kids waiting for ice cream. On our first visit, we noted that the wooden framework was up. This framework became the main structure on which our dream home was constructed. Based on that framework our bedrooms, kitchen, and family room took shape and later became a finished home.

This same concept can be applied to speaking. The information phase (Level I) is like drawing the plans and establishing the foundation of a new home. The message phase (Level II) lays out the general dimensions you'll use to frame the speech. Now it's time to put in the actual framework—the structure—that gives form to your speech and holds everything together. If you structure your speech properly, your message and information will fit—along with all the other details—into the appropriate places. With some finishing touches you'll have a complete speech.

The good news is that the structure of a successful speech is quite simple. Every great speech is built upon the familiar framework of an **introduction**, a **body**, and a **conclusion (Figure 1)**. Take it on faith that this format is the basis for success in public speaking. Now let's take a look at these structural elements in greater detail.

Introduction

The introduction is vital to the overall success of your speech. It's obviously a beginning, the place to set the tone and direction for your audience. You're asking them to take a journey with you, and like the Chinese proverb you have to begin your journey of 10,000 miles with a first step. The introduction is your first step together with your audience.

In the introduction you need to establish a bond of trust with the audience. A bond of trust is built upon authenticity. In the preceding chapter I explained that authenticity is the new paradigm for successful leadership. There is a lot of talk about credibility for a speaker, but authenticity is more important. Authenticity is what makes you believable to the audience. When your audience feels a sense of confidence and trust in you, they will be more willing to listen to what you have to say. You can earn or lose authenticity in the first few seconds of your presentation.

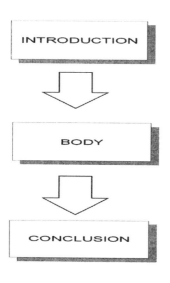

Figure 1

Reggie's Rule No. #4: Be Authentic from the Beginning. Build authenticity into your introduction. In order for your audience to perceive you as authentic your opening remarks should include the following three things:

1. Tell the audience **who you are**. This is especially important if you are speaking before a group of strangers. Why should they listen to *you*? Your introduction should provide some brief biographical information that is pertinent to the topic you are discussing.
2. Set the **tone** for your presentation.
3. Tell the audience **why you are speaking** to them. Introduce your topic and your message.

> Factoid: According to recent studies, the brain retains less information as the time of the presentation lapses. The studies show that the brain can focus its attention for up to 18 minutes of a presentation before it begins to wander off in different directions. The longer the presentation, of course, the less the brain can concentrate on what is being said. This is good information to know when it comes to timing your speech. What's the bottom line? Don't waste a lot of time on a long introduction.

Most new speakers wonder, "How long should my introduction be?" The long answer depends on the overall length of your speech, but the short answer is: short! Keep it under two minutes in a 30-minute presentation, under a minute if you can manage it. Remember, most audiences have very short attention spans. If your introduction is too long, you will lose your audience. You have between 15-30 seconds to engage them before they start to drift away from you.

Another key to introducing yourself to your audience—and building authenticity—is the use of a biography, or *bio*. When introducing yourself to the audience, relate only information that is pertinent to your subject. There's probably no need to mention you were born in a log cabin in Atlanta, GA. But here's an exception. What if you are speaking to the Convention of Southern Homemakers? Your personal connection will give them the sense that you are someone from their neck of the woods. You can build a bridge with a common heritage in the south. If you have a connection, great! Otherwise, your bio serves to assure the audience that you have the credentials to speak on the subject you have chosen.

It's a good idea to spend some time developing a bio, though it may not be easy. We're often too busy living our lives to really reflect on all that we have done. We are too busy looking at what we don't have; we forget all the things we do have. I think you'll find that putting together a bio is a great way for you to see on paper your experiences and skills. From the breadth and depth of your experiences and professional competencies you will find much rich material you can use in your opening remarks.

EXERCISE #3

Making Your Bio

To get you started, a tip sheet is provided on the following page. I want you to think hard about these things before you answer them. I suggest you document your responses. At this point please don't edit it. Just put down everything that comes to mind. Don't worry about spelling or grammar. Concentrate on the content. It's a valuable exercise, so do it now!

Make a copy of the bio tip sheet. Fill in the answers in the spaces provided. If the space is too small to write in your answer, then write the answer on a another piece of paper. Make sure to put the question number next to the answer. Spend as much time as you need to answer the questions. I would suggest that after you fill in the answers, you return to the sheet later to review the questions again. Feel free to add whatever biographical information you think is important. These questions are meant only to draw out your life experiences, you can add any additional information you feel would benefit your listeners.

Biography Tip Sheet

1. Where were you born?

2. Where did you grow up?

3. List your educational experience

4. List your work experience

5. What are your hobbies?

6. What is the most exciting experience you've ever had?

7. What do you consider your strengths/weakness?

8. What is the one thing that you think people would be surprised to learn about you?

9. What is your dream in life?

10. If money were not an object, what would you be doing in life?

11. List the five most important things that have happened to you.

12. What are your most significant achievements?

Now that you have recorded your responses, you are ready to create your master bio. From this master you can create many bios, depending on your topic and your audience. Use the same process to create a speech to create your bio. The bio should have a goal (see Level I). Use the techniques under Developing Your Message (Level II) to get your bio ready, write it out in outline form.

You now have a template for constructing an introductory bio. Once you know your topic, look into your master bio to identify information that is relevant to the topic. If you have chosen to talk about leadership in a corporate environment, then pull out your bio examples of leadership. Make these examples the core of your introductory bio.

You can create as many bio introductions as you have topics to discuss. This will help keep your material fresh. If you speak before the same group more than once, you can share different aspects of your life experiences. The bio helps establish your identity and authenticity. It is your way to shape how the audience is going to perceive you.

Yet your bio should be brief. You just want to give the audience a little taste of what is to come. You want to whet their appetite, so it is important to give it a lot of thought.

On the other hand, if possible, have someone else introduce you. This allows someone else to brag about your accomplishments and speak to your credentials. It is always better to let someone else blow your horn. When introduced by someone else, do not leave what they say up to chance. Make sure the person who is introducing you is good at introductions and is going to tell the audience the things you want them to know about you. Better still, write up your own introduction. This will ensure that the audience hears everything that needs to be said about you. Of course, a bio introduction is not necessary if the audience already knows you.

Effective Openings

An effective opening sets the stage for your entire speech. It puts the audience in the proper frame of mind to listen to what you have to say. An effective opening will accomplish three objectives.

1. Grab the attention of the audience
2. Show the benefits the audience will derive from the presentation
3. Establish that you are qualified to speak on the subject

I am a believer in grabbing the audience's attention from the beginning. Statistics show that that you have 15 seconds to bring your audience into focus or else you will lose them. It's a good idea to get them involved mentally right from the very beginning of your speech. Immerse your audience in your subject as soon as possible. You want to drop your audience right into the middle of the action. It's the technique that is used in suspense thrillers and action adventure movies. The writers and directors start off the first scene by putting you in the middle of the action. Here's how you can get your audience in the middle of the action.

Attention-Getting Techniques

Ask a Question. The question you ask can be rhetorical or one you wish answered. A rhetorical question does not require a specific answer, but should be phrased for maximum impact. An example might be, "Did you know that one-sixth of the world's population lives on less than $1.00 a day?" It's a rhetorical question because it is framed in such a way that an answer is not required. You are putting something before your audience that perhaps they are unaware of, or hadn't thought of in the way you're suggesting. You might follow up with another question, such as, "Could you live on less than $1.00 a day?" Now you have involved your audience. You have opened their minds and hearts for your message.

The other way to use a question is to actively seek a response from your audience, In effect, the audience becomes part of the presentation. This can be a dangerous area for a public speaker to enter. Why? The problem is that the question may be answered in such a way that it throws you off from what you were prepared to discuss. I have seen this happen to many good speakers. Fortunately, most were professionals who knew how to get themselves out of a sticky situation. But since you are reading my book, I assume you have not had such extensive training and are not a professional speaker. But there are some simple ways to overcome this danger.

You can assure the appropriate answer by having a person set up to answer the question. This is something that is done quite frequently in political campaigns. The audience is peppered with individuals who have been given questions to ask the candidate. The candidate has been prepped to answer the questions. You can have someone set up to answer the question in the way you wish. You're stimulating audience participation, and it will help move your speech forward—in the direction you choose. Try not to view this as manipulative, but as discretionary assistance that will benefit your listeners.

My personal belief is that it is best to allow your regular audience to answer the question. That way you get real participation from your audience. This really gets them involved and they will want to listen to how you are going to handle the topic. If you are going to do this, spend a lot of time formulating the question you'll be asking. Frame your question in a way to make it crystal clear for your audience to answer.

What makes for a good question for your audience? The question should be framed so that the answer will fit in with your material. Make sure you do your homework on the audience so that you understand how they will respond to your question. Here are a few simple things you can do to ensure an appropriate response. Ask questions in which the audience:

- shares a common knowledge of the subject
- shares a common experience
- gives a simple Yes/No answer that supports your speech

How would you apply these rules to asking an effective question? If you are talking to men, you might try to frame a question around a sports theme, such as, "How many of you would love to play basketball like Michael Jordan?" You might appeal to the shared experience of a group; perhaps they're all mountain climbers or real estate brokers. Frame your question around their shared experience. Problems can surface if the questions are open ended.

There's too much room for different interpretations. That's one of the reasons why I like the simple yes-or-no format.

Yes-or-no questions are wonderful to put before your audience. They are simple, but still require a certain level of thought. You still need to frame them or else you might wind up with the wrong answer to your question. Some of the best ones I have heard have been set up so that no matter what the answer, yes or no, the speaker was ready to use the answer in the presentation.

For example, "Do you believe in the death penalty?" Whatever the answer, the speaker can build upon it. If you were to give a speech in favor of the death penalty and the answer to the question from an audience member was yes, then you can go smoothly into your speech. But what if you received a negative response? You acknowledge the answer by noting that there are many sincere people who feel the same way as the person who answered the question. Maybe this is a good time to examine the opposite side to that answer to see if there are benefits to having a death penalty. It's not very hard to do. You just need to make sure that you are prepared to acknowledge different viewpoints in the subject and use that to segway to the prospective you will be discussing.

My wife and I got tricked into one of those time share vacation give-away programs where you go and listen to their program for an hour, and then they spend two hours twisting your arm about signing up. The approach was terrible. They spent most of their time trying to figure out how much money we had, and then convincing us that with our lifestyle and economic status, we would be fools not to buy a time-share. What's the lesson from this? Their approach didn't match their audience.

This is another example of why it is important to know your audience. If I were giving a speech on time-shares, I would never talk about money. I would start off by asking the audience, "Do you like to take vacations? Raise your hand." Then I would ask the audience, "Would you like to take more vacations for less money?" The answer would be yes. Now the audience is with me. Then I would make the presentation, showing how my time-share program will provide them with all of the things that they look for in a vacation.

You can test the question. If you arrive early you can go around and ask your question to the audience. What is the reaction? Or, you can ask some friends or colleagues. But remember, audience response can change. Demographics—the makeup of the audience—can change the answer to the question. Still, a good question is an excellent way to kick start the introduction.

Give an Illustration. Another way is to start off with an illustration. An illustration can add a lot of power to your speech. An effective illustration makes a comparison between two ideas intended to draw parallels in the minds of audience members. You might start off by saying that business is a lot like football. Both are full contact sports. That's a good illustration. A good illustration should draw a picture in the mind of listeners. Here are a few tips that can help you do that:

- Use illustrations about:
  - Family
  - Hometown
  - Current/former workplaces
- Choose an illustration that requires movement of your body
- Paint a picture, use vivid descriptions
- Use props, or visual aids, for the illustration

This is a perfect place to use your own imagination. The key is to make the illustration simple to grasp, and to use everyday images that will be familiar to your listeners. A powerful illustration is a wonderful attention-grabbing technique.

Tell a Story. You can start off your speech with a story. Telling a story is also a very powerful way to get your audience to believe in you. Everybody likes to hear a good story. I list the use of stories as a **Power Technique**. Check out the **Power Techniques** section of this book to learn how to weave a good story. Use the story to get your audience's attention.

Tell a Joke.. You can take the funny bone approach and tell a **joke**. Humor should be part of most presentations. It is not used very much because most people don't know how to employ it. It can also be a very dangerous technique, so proceed with caution. If the humor is inappropriate it will likely turn off some or all of the audience before you even have a chance to get to the message. Even appropriate humor can be difficult. What goes over in one group may not be a hit in another. Before you think about using humor as a part of your introduction, there are many factors to consider. Again, check out the **Power Techniques** section of the book for all the things you need to think about before employing humor. Humor is potentially a good way to prepare your audience for your message. But just like any other technique, the humor should fit the topic. Don't use a joke just because it is funny; use it because it fits your topic.

Don't allow yourself to get stuck using just one introduction. Use a variety of introductions. The list I have given is not exhaustive. Think of it as a template from which you can design your own introductions. You can even combine them together. The key is that the introduction should work to get your audience acquainted with you and put them in the mood to want to listen to what you have to say.

Body

If you introduced your subject properly, then the body of your speech should flow from your introduction like a stream of water. The body is the bulk of your speech. The body is the place where you give the audience the information they came to hear. This is where you get to present all your hard-earned research, and to put your ideas and facts out into the world.

This is the place where you insert the main points you developed in your outline. How should your information be presented? There is quite a bit of debate in the speaking world about this particular subject. There are many ways to present your information. I will provide some general principles and examples of how they can be employed. Be creative: What's the best way to serve up this information to your audience?

I suggest you present the body of your speech in a clear, logical format. The human mind is hardwired to recognize patterns. A speech that follows a logical path will establish a pattern. You can take advantage of the ability of our minds to look for patterns. Let me give you an example. Take a look at a modern TV comedy show. Many people think sitcoms are new and innovative, but they are not. The concept of the comedy show can be traced back to the Greek comedies. The Greek comedies were just the same in their format as today's half hour sitcom. They recognized the patterns. And when these patterns are followed with some innovation and fresh thinking, the results can be remarkable.

Take advantage of patterns in human thinking. For instance, let's say you want to convince your audience to recycle. In the introduction, you could say, "Today I am going to explain to you the three most important reasons why we should recycle our trash. The first reason is . . ."

Then you would go through each reason. Can you see how the pattern has been set? You mention the three reasons in the beginning. Then you use the body to discuss each of the three points.

It is important to break down your speech into main subject areas. The subject areas should be supportive of the overall theme of the material you will be discussing. Each subject should be treated like a mini-theme. It should have it's own introduction, body, and closing. It's sort of a speech within a speech. I find it is helpful to keep the main points down to three if possible, but no more than five. The human mind will not be able to hold on to more than five major subject areas delivered in one dose. Besides, you only have five fingers to hold up to show them anyway! Maybe that's how God wanted it to be.

The body should provide your audience with all the information they need. You are making your presentation of the facts. Laying out the facts in a logical, coherent manner is the best way to present information. Think about the needs of your audience. What kind of questions do they need answered? How can you convince them—or persuade them—with your arguments?

One approach that I find most helpful is the funnel method. Think of your speech as a funnel. If the funnel is upside down, with the narrow spout being on top, then you are taking the narrow-to-wide position. Here, you provide very little information up front about the subject. As you develop the information, you begin to give your audience a bigger picture. When you turn the funnel around (Figure 2), you provide a lot of information at the beginning, and then narrow down near the end. Figure 2 is an example of wide-to-narrow organization.

General Information

Detailed Information
Figure 2

Suppose you are presenting information about our nation being overweight. You can start off by saying we are the fattest nation on earth. If our kids played more sports, it could cut down on obesity. You talk about the importance of playing sports in a child's life. You say that in your county children's sports are not being well supported by the community. A particular sport that would require a minimum amount of financial support would be soccer. Parents provide the uniforms and volunteers and local government provides the facilities. See the progression? We went from a wide topic of an overweight nation to a narrow solution of kids playing soccer.

Detailed Information

Now reverse it (Figure 3). We talk about having neighborhood soccer clubs for children. Parents provide volunteers and the local government provides the facili-

General Information
Figure 3

ties. Sports can play a significant role in a child's life. It can cut down on childhood obesity. It can also help improve the future health of our entire nation. Get the point? You have turned the funnel upside down, giving a little information up front, and then you open it up to helping our entire nation.

The funnel approach is a very natural way of presenting information. The key is that it follows the way we think. But I believe there are as many approaches out there as there are people. That's why it is important to know your audience and then work your presentation to the audience listening style. Sometimes, this will not be possible. I have given you general principles that should work regardless of the audience. These are time-honored ways of getting the information to your audience.

Conclusion

Every effective speech needs a powerful conclusion, and I emphasize "needs." Unfortunately, many presenters fail to make a powerful close. Oh yes, they say they are finished, or they say thank you. But that is not a conclusion, that's an exit. A great speech deserves a great conclusion.

What makes a great conclusion? You want to leave something for your audience to think about, meditate on, or take some sort of action. After all, why speak if you were not interested in your audience being stimulated to act in a certain way with the information you have just given them? The question is, what exactly is it that you want the audience to do?

When formulating your speech, I asked you to establish a goal for the speech. As I stated earlier, the goal is not the same as the message. The goal is what you expect the audience to do with the information you have given them. It is at the conclusion of your speech that you clarify what is the goal of the speech.

For example, if your speech has dealt with recycling, you have shown all the ways in which recycling can be done. You have shown how recycling saves money, energy, and protects the environment. Now it's time to invite your audience to recycle. It should be as simple as, "Now get out there and recycle, and save our planet!"

The conclusion does not have to be used exclusively as a clarion call for action. The conclusion can be used to ensure that the audience understood the information you presented. You can use your conclusion to drive home your main points. At the end of the speech, you can recount the major subject areas, highlighting the main areas of argument. When it comes to remembering, repetition is the key. Your conclusion is the place where you can make it stick.

For instance, to make my main point memorable I might say these words to the audience: "Well, if you don't remember anything else that I have said this afternoon, I want you to remember . . ." Get the point? Here you have re-focused audience attention on the one point you want them to remember. It serves as a mental sticky note in their brains. The conclusion is your last chance to make your points to the audience. This is the place where you'll make them remember you or wish they could forget you. So plan the conclusion to reinforce the message and the goal.

To help you keep track of all this, I have included a worksheet on the next page. You are welcome to use it to put together your information.

Topic:

Presentation Goal:

Presentation Message:

Introduction/Time:

Body/Main Points/Time:

Conclusion/Time:

Main Structure of a Speech

A. Introduction - 30-60 seconds. An introduction should…
  1. Grab the attention of the audience
  2. Tell the audience who you are
  3. Tell the audience why they should listen to you

B. Body - Main focus of your presentation. This is where you present your facts. The body should be clear and logical.

C. Conclusion - Short and to the point. The conclusion should…
  1. Summarize your main points
  2. Call your audience to action
  3. Be memorable

Attention Grabbing Techniques

  A. Tell a story
  B. Tell a joke
  C. Give an illustration
  D. Ask a thought provoking question

LEVEL IV
PREPARATION

"To get in practice of being refused."

Diogenes Laertius, on being asked why he was begging for alms from a statue, Lives of the Philosophers

One sign of a good chef is that the kitchen is organized before the meal is prepared. All the utensils and ingredients have been placed where they will be needed. Everything has been organized ahead of time because delivering a delectable masterpiece requires split-second timing. There's no time for fumbling around, and very little room for error. It is no different when it comes to presenting your information to your audience. Before you begin to speak, you must first prepare yourself.

In thinking about how to make your presentation great, remember **The Five Ps**: Proper Preparation Prevents Poor Performance. When you are not prepared to deliver your information, you tend to make mistakes. Faulty preparation will be as apparent to your audience as it is to you. You will lack the confidence you need in yourself and lose authenticity with your audience. Proper preparation determines whether or not you will serve up a great speech.

The Room

First, you need to get a feel for the room. Before you speak, you should visit the site where you will be speaking. If possible, visit the place before your speaking date. Sometimes that may not be possible; you may only have access the day of the event. If that is the only time you have, then you will have to use this time to its fullest to familiarize yourself with the environment. The following exercise will help you to get to know your environment.

EXERCISE #4

Getting to Know the Room

Pay a visit to the room where you'll be speaking. Walk around the room, look at the furnishings, and examine how the room is set up. You might even try to get some input on how the room will be set up for you. In most cases, you will not have that option. The room will be what the room is. Take a seat in one of the chairs and get a feel for what the audience will see from their seats. If you have a companion, have this person stand up in the speaking area as you observe. Take in the lighting, the look, feel, and even the smell of the room. Go to the front of the room. Go to the podium as if you are delivering your presentation. Take a moment to close your eyes and picture the room in your mind's eye. Now take another look at the room. Make sure your picture is accurate. Now take yet another snapshot. Close yours eyes again. Burn the image of the room into your mind, and then leave.

Is it a good idea to practice your speech in the same place you'll be giving it? The answer is, "Yes and no." Let's deal with the no. In the very initial stages of getting the proper words into your head, I would say that preparing in the same place where you're going to speak is not necessary. Besides, it may be logistically impossible to do. You may be limited by time constraints that will cut into your practice time.

Now let's examine the yes answer. Yes, it's always good to get a little practice in the room where you will be speaking. It will help you to become acquainted with the surroundings and give you a sense of comfort. If possible, you can practice giving your whole speech, but giving the whole speech in the room is not always necessary. I find that just giving out a few opening lines, a few main points, and then really working on giving a rousing conclusion, is enough "room" practice.

Practicing in the room where you'll be speaking is similar to what rock musicians do when they go into an auditorium for a sound check and to get a feel for the stage before the show. If it helps, think of yourself as a music superstar getting ready for the big show. Play some music if it will get you into the proper mood. Musicians perform the same show in different towns, but they recognize that each venue is different. You need to understand how to take advantage of room logistics, and how to overcome any problems created by the way the room is set up. Maybe there are blind spots in the room, or perhaps the stage lighting is not very good.

Once, as I began speaking to an audience, I noticed everyone was sitting in the back of the room; the entire front row was empty. I knew that would not work, so I went out and had the entire back row move to the front. It made the experience more memorable for all participants. I was able to do this because I understood the dynamics of the room I was speaking in, and the effect it would have on the audience to be so far away from the podium.

It is a good idea to check in with the people who set up the room. Make sure that everything you need will be there. I once did a presentation that included a DVD I wanted to show the audience. As it turned out, the room's PC could play the DVD, but it could not connect to the sound system in the room. I could forget about any sound. I was mortified. But fortunately I had followed **Reggie's Rule #5: Always Have an Alternate**. I brought along the same information on a VHS tape. I was in business. I wouldn't have had the problem in the first place if I had checked the room's capabilities. I made an assumption that the PC could be connected into the sound system. If I had not brought a backup it could have been extremely embarrassing. I have included in this chapter a Room Set Up Checklist that will help you avoid these problems. I have also added a Day of Event Checklist to use on the day of your presentation. This list is a lifesaver. Make a copy and keep it with you for every presentation.

Let's get back to practicing at home. My suggestion is to find a quiet place where no one will interrupt you, a place where you will feel comfortable. Make sure that there is room for you to move around and a place where you can place your notes. Find something to serve as a temporary podium. I have piled up old boxes, or even used a TV or stereo stand. At this stage, you want to be alone. Since you are just getting started, you don't need any critics around. They will get in the way of what you are trying to accomplish. We will bring in an audience later in the process.

It is important to set the appropriate atmosphere. Turn off anything that may distract you during the session. Shut off the TV, radio, or other electronic equipment. If you share your home with others, make sure to let them know that you do not wish to be disturbed. If the room has a door, shut it. Although I have been speaking to groups for almost 20 years, I still feel a little sheepish when it comes to practicing. I do my preparation work in the basement when my family is not around to disturb me. The key is to remove all distractions.

Start with your outline and your notes. Review the goals and the message in your mind again. Think about the tone that you want to set. Is it serious or funny? Maybe it's a little of both? Think about your audience. What do you want them to do? How do you want the audience to feel about you and about this material? You're now prepared to get prepared.

Preparing Your Mind

You have prepared the atmosphere and environment. Now it's time to prepare your mind for the work ahead. Clear your mind of all the concerns of the day. Don't think about what went wrong with the job, or how your spouse is driving you crazy. Remove all the frustrations and complications of the day completely from your mind. The only thing you should be thinking about is the speech you are about to deliver.

For the first step of the process, I want you to close your eyes and concentrate on your audience. If it all possible, you should have visited the place where you're going to speak. Now I want you to visualize that you are there. Imagine seeing the chairs, the curtains, and the equipment. You can see the faces of your audience. They are happy to see you. They are ready and anxious to hear what you have to say. If you did not get to visit the room where you will be speaking, just imagine what you think the room will look like, and then go through the exercise. When you are ready, open your eyes.

So what are you going to say? In the previous section of this book, you already worked out what you are going to say to your audience. Now is the time to say it out loud. Act as if you are now speaking to the audience. Since the introduction is about one to two minutes, you should not have to look at your notes. Instead, try to look out at your imaginary audience. Look at the smiles on their faces as you open with your joke. See the warm look as they are enjoying your opening story. Watch how their faces burn with curiosity as you awaken their minds with your rhetorical question. Visualize these images and record them in a mental picture while you are speaking. Do this several times for your introduction.

I really want you to practice the introduction—out loud— over and over again. Your family will probably think you are losing your mind. You may want to explain to them that you are practicing your speech out loud, not just talking to yourself. Once you feel comfortable with the introduction, move on to repeating your closing over and over.

Reggie's Rule #6 is relevant here: **The Exception Rule.** Remember that any rule can be broken, but you need a good reason for breaking it. I suggest you memorize your opening and closing, but as for the main body of your speech, don't memorize it. So you get to break a rule! Why? Remember that the opening is the place where you have to grab your audience's attention right away. You only have 15-30 seconds to get your message across. You want to make sure that your words are carefully chosen and well rehearsed. As for the closing, these are the last words you will speak to the audience. This is the place to make your point and call the audience to action. It is very important that your words in the closing are precise and to the point. So these are the two places where you should memorize the words.

Here's a technique for memorizing openings and closings. Pretend to be an actor. When a good actor speaks, we can't tell that the lines are memorized. Why? The actor makes the words her own. Now, this should be a lot easier for you, since you are not going to be reading lines written by someone else. Picture the words in your head, and then speak them in the way you would want them to be said. You will be memorizing the lines that you have written. The words should sound just like something you would say.

What about the rest of your material? Many untrained speakers are overly concerned with memorizing every word they plan to say. This is a big mistake. If you become too wrapped up in the words, then you can be easily thrown off in your speaking. If you forget a word or drop a sentence, you may find yourself looking up at the ceiling, or rubbing your head trying to remember the exact phrases or words you were *supposed* to say. In the early years of our lives, that was how we were taught to learn things. We would learn history by remembering dates or names or places. It's called *rote* learning. Unfortunately, a lot of rote learning still goes on in our schools. Now don't get me wrong, there is a place for it. But there's no place for it in public speaking.

So it's time to *unlearn* what you have learned. Your teachers taught you to memorize words and then regurgitate them on a test. And, being a well-trained kid, you were rewarded for having a good memory. But in order to really learn something, it has to become a part of you. You have to experience it, immersing yourself with the material in order to get its full meaning. It's a different learning paradigm than the one you may have grown up with.

Since you are not going to memorize the body of your speech, how is it possible to deliver the information? Let's go back to the real basics. Before we humans had a written language to express ourselves, we spoke with pictures. The earliest records we have of human communication are pictures carved or painted onto the walls of caves. In reality, words are just a symbolic representation of pictures. Don't believe it? Let's take a test. Close your eyes. Say, "Car," "Woman," "Man," "Dog." Okay, what happened? You saw them in your mind, right? Isn't that amazing? You can't even utter the words without the pictures forming in your mind.

This method of retaining knowledge has become so popular that it is even being used to teach people foreign languages. Instead of putting words on paper and having people repeat them, some language immersion classes are using images that allow people to associate the foreign word with the actual object. So instead of saying in your mind, "Señor means 'sir' in Spanish," the image of a man instantly appears in your mind when you say, "señor." No translation into English is necessary. This is a powerful tool.

Another way to boost memory and retention is with the use of *association*. Various professionals have made a lucrative living by teaching people how to remember anything by using association. In as little as 10 minutes, people have been able to recall all 50 states in the union in precise order. It seems like magic, but it is not. It is the simple technique of using pictures. You see, your mind can process images faster than it can process spoken or written words. Rather than memorizing the abstract words that represent an image, you *visualize* the image itself.

The same concept can be applied to retaining the information you need to deliver to your audience. You have to learn how to convert your words into images, which are easier to recall. These images will act as cues so that you will say the right thing at the right time.

You have already taken the first vital step toward visualization. Your outline does not contain any specific phrases or words that you're going to use. (I will be using the words "notes" and "outlines" interchangeably from this point forward.) If you've generated certain facts, these have been written into your notes. Facts might be figures, dates, or specific numbers that you may need to keep written down. Your outline is the framework upon which to build the visualization process. Make sure that the notes you have are legible, large enough to be seen, and are written on note cards. You can use a sheet of paper if you like, but I prefer cards for their durability and the convenience of being able to put them away quickly. Also, I suggest making a copy on your computer so that you will have a backup. Once I lost my notes, but someone was able to email them to me.

With your notes before you, look at the first main point you will be making. Take time to think about it. What would you like to say about this particular point? What if you were discussing this with a good friend: How you would explain your position on this point? Now go ahead and have a conversation with your invisible friend. Tell him how you feel about this point, and what is it that your friend needs to understand. Make it like any normal conversation. Now take some more time to think about it, and then try it all over again.

As you go through this process, the appropriate words will begin to form in your mind. Move from having a conversation with your friend to seeing your audience. What is their reaction to what you are saying? How can you change your words to make your message have more impact? Can you replace passive phrases with more active words, words that give a sense of action or forward momentum? At this point, listen very closely to the phrases and words that are pouring out of your head. Say them out loud. How do they sound? Does it sound like something you would say? Do the words fit together?

This is not easy. Sometimes it is hard to come up with the words. Public speaking is an art. It's just like painting or songwriting. It requires the controlled release of creative juices. You may or may not be comfortable with the creative process. So what happens if you are blocked up creatively, or have difficulty coming up with the words or the exact idea you want to express? Well, I have a novel idea for you; it's different from what you have been told in school. STOP!! Stop thinking about it. Go outside and take a walk around the neighborhood. Smell the roses. Go to the gym. Call up your mother. Hug somebody. You'll return to your work with a different perspective, a whole new way of looking at things. You need to release the tension that is blocking you from being creative.

One way that public speaking differs from the art of writing is that, when speaking, you can plagiarize techniques. Have you seen a public speaker do something that really jazzed you up? Then repeat what that speaker did, but with your own touch. Think of a more creative way you could do it. How can you improve upon it? Take that and use it in your presentation. Now, get yourself back to your muse.

Once you have the words, do not write them down. Writing down the words you want to say is like using a crutch. Crutches are for those whose limbs are too weak to carry them. Through the course of this book, we have strengthened your limbs so that you are no longer in need of crutches. Now is the time to visually associate the words you wish to say with your outline. Do this by adding *key words* to your outline.

What is a key word? A key word is a cue to what you are going to say to your audience. For example, during the course of your speech, you are going to tell the story of how you took your dog to a vet. Your key words might be Vet/Dog. These words would instantly trigger in your mind the image of taking your dog to the vet, and the words will come to you out of your head. There will be no hesitation as you simply describe to your audience the images freely flowing from your mind. And you can describe it in the same way every time because that's how your mind has stored the information. You no longer have to remember a jumble of phrases or images; you only need to tie key words to the images already stored in your mind.

Are you worried about forgetting something? Forget about it! Your mind has an infinite capacity to store information. We use less than one percent of our brainpower. There's enough gray matter up there to store a million speeches with room to spare. So don't worry about forgetting anything. You won't forget what you want to say if you follow this method you're learning today.

Apply this method to all the points on your outline. This is the time where you are bringing all the puzzle pieces together. I find it helpful to apply this method systematically. I start at the first main point and work my way down until I reach the conclusion. I make sure that everything sounds right and fits into its proper place. This is also a time for discovery. As you are actually saying the words, you may find certain words that looked good on paper just don't sound good in real life. So you may have to do some adjusting.

Another danger you may find is that you are running short of time. You may have too much information. What do you do? Go back to the essential models we spoke about in the beginning. Remember what your goal is. What are you trying to accomplish? What does your audience need to know? Remove any extraneous material that does not meet the main criteria you established at the beginning of the process. I have found that this works every time.

What if you have the opposite problem? You have too much time and not enough material. Go back to the information-gathering phase. There should be plenty of material that you chose not to use in the presentation. Take a second look; some of this material can now be included. If you can't get the material to stretch, consider using illustrations or stories to fill the remaining time. But remember, the stories or illustrations must be related to your topic. This is an opportunity to use the extra time to elaborate on the main points. Another option is that you could open the floor to questions. Beware, this could be dangerous if you are not prepared. Make sure you remember to read the **Power Tips** section on Questions.

What if you are still short on time? If you can make your point and get your call for action done in less than the allotted time, there is no rule that says you have to use up all your time. You *can* end your presentation early. Most speakers tend to go overtime, so ending your speech early could buy you some appreciation points from your audience. I was once given ten minutes for a technical presentation. My boss was appalled when I told him I could do it in five minutes. He felt that I needed the entire ten minutes. I explained to him that most of the technical presenters used up their allotted time and then some. If I presented this under time, they would love it. Well I did it, and it was a hit. It garnered me an overwhelming applause. And it secured my fame in the organization as someone who knows how to deliver information to management in a timely and effective manner. It is a good reputation for you to build for yourself.

Practicing on Your Own

Feeling confident, eh? Are you thinking that it's Miller™ time? Not so fast. Now it's time to go over it again and again. And just when you think you can't do it one more time, do it again. Now your main session is over, but the practice sessions will still continue. Whenever you have free time, I want you to think about delivering this speech. Maybe you are waiting in line at a retail store, or maybe waiting to pick up the kids from soccer practice. Or it's after lunch, and you're sitting quietly at a table, or perhaps taking a leisurely afternoon stroll around the neighborhood. This is the time when you will etch the entire speech into your mind. When the quiet moments come, you are going to pull out the speech and go over it again and again.

You do need to practice using your notes, and having your notes close by during the presentation is a good idea. Here are a few pointers on how to use your notes during the presentation:

- Use 3x5 index cards. Write large letters for better visibility.
- Look at your notes when starting a new point. Before completing the point, look for the next point in the outline.
- Keep notes straight in front of you. Adjust podium/lectern so that you can glance down at your notes without moving your head. Just look down with your eyes.

But hold on. I don't want you to use the note cards just yet. I just want you to work on the speech in your head. Use the note cards only if you need a memory cue. Practice very hard on your introduction and conclusion. Don't look at your notes during the introduction and conclusion. These are times to fully engage your audience. Your notes will get in your way, and you'll become self-conscious. So practice your speech without notes whenever you can, but I would advise that when in a public place, you should say the speech in your head, not out loud. People may think you are crazy. You don't want to be arrested *before* you deliver your speech.

Here are a few points that you can work on in your head. I call this silent practicing:

- Opening
- Closing
- Main key points
- Stories
- Jokes
- Illustration/comparison

As you go through this exercise, you will begin to notice that your speech begins to take on a life of its own. You will begin to create what I call the *flow*. The flow is best described as a rhythm that begins to run through your entire speech. Your words flow easily from your mouth like music from an instrument. In your mind the images are racing ahead and you have a feeling of confidence in yourself and your material. As the saying goes, you know the material as well as you know the back of your hand.

Now that you know what you are going to say, it's time to incorporate some physical and voice presence techniques into your speech, which I discuss in the next chapter. When you are working on your presence, it is important that you make these techniques look natural. So don't spend a lot a time trying to remember every gesture or voice inflection. If you have worked hard on getting into the flow of the speech, the physical and voice presence will come naturally into the places where they are needed. If you have completed the proper preparation as discussed earlier in this chapter, then these techniques will not appear forced, mechanical, or artificial, but will appear as a natural outgrowth of your presentation. Remember, the key is to relax.

It is also important that you take on the persona of the effortless speaker. The speech should not appear to be a speech. What am I talking about here? I am saying you should make your speech appear like a conversation. The only difference is that you are having a conversation with a larger audience. The conversational approach will make you feel more relaxed and will gain you rapport with your audience.

Conversational style speaking is not stilted, wordy, or artificial. These are the three deadly sins when it comes to being boring. On the other hand, you don't wish to appear too relaxed or casual.

You may then become careless in your vocabulary or start using poor posture. So the good speech is somewhere a little above a conversation you would have with a close friend, but it would not be on the level of the President's State of the Union address. It is important that you make your audience feel comfortable with you or you will lose their attention.

Now practice the key points that we mentioned in the last few paragraphs. Get into the **flow** through the use of your key words and images to keep the speech in motion and make a smooth presentation. Use your **presence** to punch up the material and give it a life of its own. This will give your speech its individuality, making it different from any other speech.

It is important to practice with the equipment you are going to use during your presentation. Are you giving a multimedia presentation? Be sure to make time to practice your presentation with the equipment. I recommend practicing in the place where the event is going to be held. If that is not possible, then set up the equipment in a suitable substitute location.

In practice sessions, you should work on how to keep the focus on what you are saying and not allow your equipment to distract from the presentation. A multimedia presentation should enhance what you are saying, not take away from it. Please review my Visual Aids section. It is located in the **Power Techniques** section. This will give you insight on how to present a powerful presentation using visual aids.

Once I was booked to give a speech on the exact same subject the speaker before me had given. Even the background material was the same used by the previous speaker. The person who booked me had failed to check that my speech was different. Although it was essentially the same information, the audience reaction was phenomenal. They loved it and told me so after I completed the speech. My presentation of the material was totally different than the previous speaker. It was refreshing, exciting, and it really captured their attention. Billions of humans live on the earth, all of us have hands and fingers, but each fingerprint is different and unique. So it is with your speech and your presence. Your presence will set you apart from anyone who goes before you or who will follow you. The idea is that you want to make that personal presentation a positive memory.

Getting Feedback

Now you are ready for the critics. Now it's time to let someone else hear that speech. Even professionals have to try out their material somewhere. If you have done this long enough and understand the essential elements to the point where they are a part of you, then your first practice for your audience can be in front of your audience. That's where I get out any minor kinks and improve it. But if you are not at that level of confidence and skill, I suggest you find a person or a group of people to listen to it before you deliver it. Feedback is important at this point in the preparation process.

Who should listen to your speech? A spouse is good, or a significant other. But be careful: Not all the advice they give you will be good advice. Remember that speaking is an art, not a science, which means that reactions to your speech will be subjective. Opinions may vary as to your strong and weak points. I have devised a way of removing that variable if you are going to have someone who is not a trained public speaker review your speech.

I have created a chart that lists some essential physical elements of public speaking (Figure 1). People can rate you from one to five. Five is the best, and one means you need to improve significantly. Also, there is an area for them to make a brief comment. This is perfect for speaking before a group of people. Feedback is immediate, and in a written form that can be preserved for future reference. You may find certain patterns in your speaking, good and bad, which need attention. This sheet will help to remove some subjectivity and give your sample audience a guideline to follow when observing the presentation.

Above all, you want to make sure that the speech flows and that they understand the main points you are making. Is your introduction an attention grabber? Are you saying anything that could be perceived as inappropriate, inaccurate, or not standing the test of logic? Have them listen to ensure that your delivery is conversation-

Circle one for each category
1 - Needs Improvement
2 - Fair
3 - Good
4 - Excellent
5 - Outstanding

Category	Rating	Comments
Posture:	1 2 3 4 5	
Gestures:	1 2 3 4 5	
Eye Contact:	1 2 3 4 5	
Facial Expression:	1 2 3 4 5	
Body Movements:	1 2 3 4 5	

Figure 1

al. Also, you can use the sample audience to practice your eye contact and use of notes. If possible, have a trained speaker review the
speech. Unfortunately, this is not always possible, and the majority
of people who speak are not trained—and do not do it very well. But
there are places that you can turn to for assistance. I list them in the
back of the book. The best place is Toastmasters International. It is
an association devoted to creating excellent public speakers. Their
members are trained to evaluate other speakers in a positive and

informative manner. I joined Toastmasters several years ago and I benefited from all the positive comments. If you join the club, you can give your speech there and be evaluated by a trained public speaker. If someone in your organization belongs to Toastmasters, ask that person to listen to your speech. Make sure this person has been in the organization for some time, and that the person is an active member who is giving and evaluating speeches.

The other possibility is to hire a speech coach. A speaking coach can be an invaluable aid when it comes to getting your message across to an audience. I guess my prejudice will begin to show here, since *I am a professional speaking coach*. Why should you use a speaking coach? A speaking coach is trained to recognize what makes a great speech. A speaking coach will evaluate your speaking skills, look at your strong and weak points. The coach will work with you one-on-one to accent your strong points and play down your weak ones. With individual attention, you will begin to progress more rapidly in your delivery. Your progress will be more visible to those around you. The speech coach will customize a specific program to deal with your particular issues and will act as a private evaluator of your progress. If the message is important, and speaking is going to be your way to move to the top of the organization, then you should give serious thought to employing a speech coach at some point in your career. The benefits will last a lifetime.

If you don't have or want a sample audience, but wish to polish your speech before you present it to your actual audience, there are two more options available. First, you can record your speech on a tape recorder. I have to plead guilty that this is something I have found hard to do. Most of us are somewhat put off by the sound of our own voice and we get caught up in listening to it and feeling bad. But if you listen long enough, you will get over those negatives and hear the words you are saying and how you are saying them. With tape recording you can make sure that you have flow, correct pronunciation, and that you are utilizing the full gamut of voice presence to get through to your audience. Also, it's a good memory aid. Playing your speech over and over again will help lock it into your mind.

Another reviewing option is videotape. Thanks to the technological wonders of our age, most homes have a video camera. If you don't have one, you can borrow one from your Aunt Kathy. The great advantage of a video camera is that it can capture everything. You can bring together both the voice and physical presence on tape where you can look for places to improve. With videotape, you can send it out for review and feedback. Even if they can't be with you, they can see it for themselves. When I say videotape, I am also including digital camcorders and other media that can be used to record video and sound. A videotape can also be used to show others what you can do. Video is an excellent medium to examine yourself. I recommend using videotape at some point in your public speaking.

Now that you have your feedback, what are you going to do with it? Review it very carefully. Don't be overly concerned if the feedback appears to be negative in a number of areas. Actually this can be a very good thing. You don't want your evaluators to gloss over the parts they did not like because they were afraid of hurting your feelings. Feedback is not criticism; it is a mechanism for improving what is already a good presentation. You are moving your presentation from good to great. So welcome the feedback with open arms and an open mind. If you have used multiple evaluators, look for the trends in what they are saying. In the trends you will find the rough gems you need to polish up, or the diamonds, which are already shining.

Work on the points that were highlighted by your evaluators. Practice making the improvements. If they have the time, have them listen to your corrections on the spot. If time is pressing, work on the points, then let them view the new presentation on their own time. The advantage of this is that they get to see a whole new presentation with their ideas and feelings incorporated. This will make the presentation appear fresh and new to their eyes and may even generate some new ideas for how you can present the material. Feedback is a powerful tool—always seek it. I have devoted an entire **Power Technique** to discuss the importance of feedback. Make sure you read it.

It is important that you have a dry run on any equipment you will be using on the day of the event. Try to get into the room an hour or two before the presentation. Make sure that all the equipment needed is there and in working order. This is your responsibility. Go through a mini dry run. If you are using PowerPoint slides, make sure they can be seen with the lighting in the room. Ensure that the sound is adequate.

Now it's almost show time. If possible try to get yourself to the event room before you have to speak, so you can do a dry run. If possible, give a portion of the speech before the empty room. Of course, this may not be possible. If it is possible, then all the better. If not, then just go to the room and familiarize yourself with your surroundings once again. Go through the exercise we recommended for the first time you see the room. Then just before you speak, leave the room, and relax. Don't think about your speech any more. You've done your preparation, and you're ready to deliver an excellent speech.

Once I was giving a speech before a large crowd. When the speech was over a very nicely dressed woman approached me. She thanked me for coming and giving such a powerful presentation. She asked me how many times I had given that speech before. She wanted to know because it all seemed so easy. I told her it was my 21st time giving that speech. My wife gave me a funny look. She knew that this was the first time I had given this speech. I told my wife that it may be the first time before a human audience, but in my mind I have given that speech at least 20 times. The secret to making it look effortless was to act as if it was the 21st time I was giving the speech.

There is no "practice makes perfect" when it comes to public speaking. The idea is not to appear perfect. Attempts at a perfect speech might come off as not genuine or lacking real feeling. You are practicing to make your presentation sound less like a speech and more like a conversation with the audience. You are practicing in order to make yourself sound more natural. It's a strange concept when you think about. I mean, you sound natural all the time, right? But when you speak before a large audience on an important subject, it puts a damper on your naturalness. Everything you've been working on in this book will help restore that natural presence to you.

Presentation Title: _____

Event Date: _____ Event Time: _____

Room Set Up Checklist

- Room Configuration/Setup
- Lighting
- Proper Ventilation/Heating/Cooling
- Outlets for Electrical Power
- Setup for Audio/Visual Presentation
- Ensure Sound/Microphone Setup
- Location of Exits, Entrances, Restrooms

Day of Event Checklist:

- Audio/Visual Equipment Setup Working
- Check Microphones for Sound
- Check Room is Setup Properly
- Podium/Lectern is Present and Set Up
- Check Lighting/Heating/Cooling

Special Considerations:

Preparation:

- Check the room on the day of the event
- Use the checklist in the book
- Always have an alternate plan for glitches
- Practice at home
- Memorize only Introduction and Conclusion
- Look for feedback
- Use the feedback form

LEVEL V

DELIVERY

"The keenness of his saber was blunted by the difficulty with which he drew it from the scabbard; I mean the hesitation and ungracefulness of his delivery took off the force of his arguments."

Henry Fox , Lord Holland, speaking of Horace Walpole, Lord Orford, Memoirs of King George II, *1755*

I remember that when I was a child I purchased a toy soldier kit through the mail. Advertisements at the back of every comic book would offer 200 plastic army soldiers for $1.98. I dutifully scraped together all my allowance money until I had the full amount. I mailed the money with the order form. I eagerly waited by the mailbox, hoping that this would be the day that the postman would deliver my plastic army. How disappointed I felt each time he passed by my street and there was no mail for me! It all seemed such a waste. This was not a case of expectation postponed; it was more like an expectation that was never delivered.

When you speak in public, your audience has hopes and aspirations when they take their seats, and expectations when they are listening to you. These hopes and expectations must be respected if you are going to make an effective presentation. The listeners expect you to deliver on these expectations. At the beginning of every presentation, there is the hope that you will do just that. But when this is not met, your audience might lose confidence in you. They become frustrated because you did not satisfy their needs or wants.

Equally frustrating for them is that they have taken time from their busy schedules and you failed to deliver the goods. Yes, you did the research, prepared the information, and may even have put in a few practice sessions. But if the delivery is not made in a way that is compelling and appealing to the listener, then it all was for nothing. You have wasted your time. More importantly, your have robbed your listeners of their most valuable asset: their time. You must always respect this precious commodity that has been entrusted to you. Make your presentation spectacular, one they will not forget.

Of course, there will be those who say, "I don't need any special delivery techniques. I am just relating information. I am dealing with professionals; they know what it is that I am trying to say. They understand me. I can put this together on 3 x 5 cards in less than ten minutes. I will just read it off the paper and that's it. Tell them the facts. That's all you need, right?" Wrong.

A few years ago, CD players were just hitting the market. The real craze was the Sony Walkman™ portable CD. My wife had been talking about getting a Walkman™ for a long time. But at that time, they were over $200.00, which was a little beyond our budget. As our anniversary neared, I decided to buy the CD player. I purchased a few of my wife's favorite artists on CD to help get her collection started. I was really excited and thought she would be, too. After all, I was fulfilling one of her life's dreams. I picked up my wife from the office, and in the car I presented her with the Sony and the CDs. She appeared grateful, but she did not seem as ecstatic as I thought she would be or *should* be. She assured me that she was happy with the gift.

I noticed that when we got home, she left the CD player in the box for days. I scratched my head and wondered what went wrong. Then it came to me: It was all in the presentation. I usually had my wife's present gift wrapped, with a beautiful bow, ribbons, flowers, and a wonderful card with an endearing message. This gift was devoid of all those things. I just thought, "Well hey, it's the thing she always wanted." I had failed to meet her expectations of how she thought a real anniversary gift should be presented.

What's the lesson here? **Reggie's Rule #7 is that Perception is Reality.** It really does not matter what we think about how something should be presented. The only thing that really matters is *how the receiver feels* about the presentation. Like my wife, our listeners have certain expectations of how they should be approached. The problem is that people have grown accustomed to not being considered, which results in low expectations. If you are willing to polish up your speaking skills, you will stand head and shoulders above the crowd of speakers who plod through their presentation without a thought to how the listeners would like to be approached. Aspiring new leaders of the twenty-first century can no longer ignore this aspect of communication. We must cast away our own predispositions and learn to adapt our styles to fit the needs of the audience. Our leadership has to be able to inspire and get listeners thinking in new directions they have never before considered. You want to motivate at the level of the soul and heart. You can only do that if you are meeting the needs of the listeners and putting your own needs after their needs.

One great side benefit of improving your delivery skills is that it will make a massive difference in how you are perceived in your organization. Most people who make presentations are content to present the Sony Walkman™ in the store box. So people have become used to sitting through boring presentations. They are thinking about what they will have for lunch, or what their kids are doing, or maybe even planning their next vacation. When you come up to speak, prepared with enhanced delivery skills, they are going to sit up and take notice. They will know that this is something worth listening to. You are going to give them the wrapped gift, bow, card and throw in a bottle of champagne for good measure.

Am I teaching you these delivery skills to help you impress your listeners with your newly acquired abilities? My answer is an unabashed *yes!* What is wrong with making a good impression? Somehow we have made this a dirty concept when it should not be. We are always trying to impress someone. If you are married, when you were dating your spouse, you were trying to impress him or her. You dressed up a little more, listened a little more, fixed yourself up a little more. And if you are single, you want to make a good impression on the opposite sex. If you are going to move up in your organization, you have to make a positive impression on those who have the power to influence your career. Your mere presence in the organization generates an impression to your colleagues. Why not work to improve your presentation skills to enhance that presence into a positive image? By creating this positive persona in the eyes of your audience, you build up authenticity, which is the key to influence in any organization. The audience will be prepared to listen. That's the impression to create in the mind of your audience.

An effective delivery is more than just making a good impression. It is the foundation you have to lay first. With this foundation, you are now prepared to have your message heard with a favorable ear. Having gained the attention of your audience, this is your chance to make a call to action. To get your audience to take an action, you have to convince them, influence them, and persuade them.

Think of speaking as an iceberg. The majority of the mass of an iceberg is underwater, hidden from view. The casual observer approaching the iceberg sees only the tip of the iceberg. The delivery is just the tip of the iceberg. Underneath, hidden from observation of your listeners, is all the hard work you have to do to get you up to the stage. The audience is completely oblivious to your painstaking research, practice sessions, and many lonely, frustrating hours devoted to preparing for this one moment in time. The delivery is the epitome of all the effort and hard work. It is where you bring together your hard work and sweat equity.

And now you must make all the hard work look simple and effortless? The delivery is the place where you make the difficult seem simple. The complexity of your subject is now crystal clear and easy to understand. This is where you become an effortless speaker. How can that be done? In this section you will learn how to make your delivery of the information an event for the audience to enjoy, while at the same time meeting your goals and getting your message across. Now it's Show Time.

An entire forest of paper could be devoted to writing about how to deliver the material you so painstaking and lovingly gathered. There are many books and articles you can review. But I constructed this section to provide you with what I consider to be the most important elements to making a good delivery. I consider each of these elements to be essential to the process of making an excellent presentation. If you were to examine every great speech that has ever been given, you will find these elements at the vital core of the speech. Any speech that has motivated and influenced people to action will contain the elements that will be discussed in this chapter. These techniques are proven and have passed the test of time.

Presence

Delivery is broken down into two major subheadings: Physical presence and Vocal presence. Both are essential to giving a memorable speech. In order for delivery to work well, the speaker has to create a certain aura, or atmosphere. Every great leader has a certain aura that she creates. So it is with accomplished speakers. In this publication, I call the speaker's aura their "presence." Every good speaker has to create a presence.

What is presence? It is perhaps more appropriate to describe what presence should achieve. Along with your bio and introduction, your presence should build a bridge between you and your

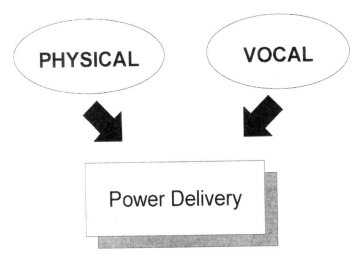

audience. The audience needs to feel they can trust and believe in what you are saying. Your presence creates the atmosphere that will gain you instant credibility. Not only should the audience feel that the words you are speaking are accurate and true, but they should also feel that you understand them as people. You are no longer just someone who is speaking. You are someone that they want to get to know. You make them feel positive about the experience and about themselves. They feel that the time they have spent listening to you was well worth the effort. That is what the results of your presence should bring to the audience.

Perhaps you feel that it is asking a lot of you. You did all the hard work to prepare for this moment and now it sounds like I am asking you to perform like an actor. But the idea here is that you want the audience to respect and trust you. They can't do that if you are mechanical or seem only to care about what you have to say. We all have been around the person who loves to talk and you can't get a word in edgewise. How uncomfortable that makes us feel! We feel disconnected to the person who is talking, and after a time we find ourselves no longer interested in what the person has to say. The same can happen to you in your presentation if your delivery does not take into account the sensitivities and feelings of your audience. It will build a barrier between them and you, a barrier that could interfere in having your message heard and understood. Your presence will remove any barrier that could come between you and transmitting your message to the audience.

All your hard work and preparation for the speech will be wasted if no thought is given to how to generate a positive experience in the minds of listeners. The message you want to communicate will be hidden if you do not learn to use appropriate delivery techniques. You must learn how to project your presence from the stage into your audience. You have two powerful vehicles you can use to deliver your presence to the audience: Vocal and Physical.

I have a very interesting statistic to present to you. Take a look at the following:

HOW WE LEARN

83%	SIGHT
11%	HEARING
3.5%	SMELL
1.5%	TOUCH
1%	TASTE

This data shows the importance of your physical presence. When it comes to your audience, 83 percent of their perception of your speech will come from non-verbal communication. This non-verbal focus means that your listeners are tuning into your physical presence. Only a mere 11 percent of perception is coming from what you are actually saying. This can be a tremendous advantage for you. It is easier to learn the physical rules of presence for effective verbal presentations than to learn many of the other aspects of public speaking. This part of the book will give you a lot of bang for your buck. Isn't it worth spending a little time on increasing your effectiveness in this area? If 83 percent of your income were coming from one client, would you not spend more time cultivating that relationship? Point made.

Physical Presence

The concept of physical presence is quite simple. It's your clothes, the way you walk, stand, gesture, and make facial expressions. As humans we are hardwired to make certain decisions based on the physical cues in our environment. When we meet people for the first time, we observe their outward appearance to ascertain something about their character. Is this person dangerous, friendly, warm, or someone we would like to get to know? All these things are swirling around in our heads.

At the same time, we make judgments about people based on all the experiences we have had in our lives. These filters in our heads are telling us what kind of person we're dealing with. Is this someone I can trust? Do I want to talk with such a person? These prejudices can be harmful, of course, especially in cases where we have stereotypical viewpoints on people who are not of our race, national origin, or religion. But on the other hand, these visual cues can be of great advantage to a speaker who is trying to gain the trust and confidence of the audience. You need to know how to get past these filters that might otherwise cause a person to tune you out. Once you bypass the filters, then your message can be heard loud and clear.

In the scope of this book, it would be impossible for me to go over every visual cue you could use to reach your audience. Besides, I find that it is better to experiment on your own. I have read a lot of material on this subject, all of which leads me to believe that there is a great deal of latitude when it comes to this area. In other words, what is sauce for the goose is not always sauce for the gander. The non-verbal communication business can be a sticky wicket, especially when you throw in cultural diversity. So I have compiled what I consider to be the necessary elements of non-verbal communication. These elements will help you deliver a speech that will command the attention of the audience and not distract them from your message.

In the non-verbal arena, we will discuss five essential, physical presence elements that can be controlled to help you effectively engage your audience. The five essential physical elements are: appearance, posture, facial expressions, gestures, and eye contact. In the following section we will define each of these elements. After that, we will discuss in detail specific techniques that you can apply to oral presentations. All of these techniques are designed to complement your verbal message with the appropriate physical message. These techniques will help open the minds of your listeners to your message.

Appearance

What is the first thing that we notice about a speaker? It's the speaker's appearance. What kind of clothes is the speaker wearing? How is she groomed? The speaker's physical presence immediately conveys a message to the audience. Is the speaker intelligent, orderly, organized, or self-confident? All of these cues are being communicated before you even have a chance to open your mouth. Your physical bearing is already sending a message to the audience. Remember you are making a presentation, and a big part of that presentation is the non-verbal cues that you send to your audience. We all want to send out the right kind of message.

It is said that, "You can't judge a book by its cover." It's a clever expression that perhaps was true in the past, but it is not true today. It is a known fact that people make their purchases based on what is on the cover of a book. Book publishers spend millions of dollars designing covers that will spur readers to buy. The cover design elements are carefully chosen to appeal to the target audiences. Most readers will spend only about 20 seconds looking at the front cover and about 10 seconds looking at the back cover before deciding to make a purchase of the book. How terrible it would be to have great content in a book, yet have an unappealing cover. The book buyer would not bother to pick up the book—much less open it and page through it—to see what you have to say. I faced the same dilemma when I put my book together, so I worked with design and marketing professionals to make the outside as enticing as the inside. They did for me what controlling your physical presence might do for your presentations: maximize your connection to your audience.

Packaging is important when it comes to selling books, because first impressions do matter. It is also important when it comes to selling yourself, your information, and your message to your audience. Your audience is trying to make the same decision that a fickle book buyer is trying to make in the bookstore. Is the information important to me? Is it worth my time/money to pay attention? Will I really benefit from what you have to say? A lot of those initial decisions will come from how you are perceived before you ever utter a word. So where do you start in your efforts to gain a favorable first impression with your audience? How do you "package" yourself to build credibility and instantly capture the attention of consumers (your audience)? You guessed it. It starts with your dress and grooming.

The professional standards for proper dress and grooming underwent radical changes in the last decade of the twentieth century. The boom of the Internet years and the entry into the work force of the Gen X'ers changed the entire working landscape. Corporate America was quick to catch the wave since it needed to buy into the talent of these young people. Suits and ties were out, jeans, clogs, and torn t-shirts were in. The mantra was that it does not matter what you look like. It was all about whether you can produce, whether you can you develop and deliver, what is demanded of you. While this was a great experiment, it is not one I suggest you indulge in when speaking in public. No matter how good your material, or how powerful your speaking skills, you still need to make an impression with your appearance. And that appearance should be designed to instill a sense of confidence in your audience.

Am I suggesting you go back to the days of blue suits, black shoes, and blue ties? No, not at all. But you do need to dress for success. What is the key for impressing your audience? The key is to know who they are. Find out about their work culture to get a good idea about how you should dress yourself. If the culture is sort of loose and casual, you may be able to experiment a little. But I still say that, for gentlemen, a suit and a tie will go a long way with an audience. The suit and tie for men still carries a meaning of authority and business in our society, while the female equivalent of the business suit does the same for women. You may be able to relax the suit if you are speaking to your book club. But even then, I would wear something a little more formal than jeans and t-shirt.

Being "well suited" not only gives positive affirmation of your credibility to your audience, but it also gives you a bit of confidence in yourself. We all seem to behave a bit differently when we are dressed up. We tend to be a little more civilized in a coat and tie. It gives us a good feeling. And that good feeling gets instantly transferred to your presentation as you look out upon your audience. I know that many women get a boost of confidence when wearing a snappy new outfit. And getting a few compliments on your wardrobe before you even begin to speak to your audience will help to boost your self-esteem, put you more at ease, and give you more confidence. So go ahead: suit up!

Posture

One sure sign of a bad speaker is poor posture at the podium. As a speaker, you should always be aware of your positioning before the audience. After the audience has looked over your clothes, your stance at the podium is the next thing they notice. How you stand at the podium or lectern sends your audience a host of signals. How you stand during your speech will communicate a lot about how you feel about your subject matter, how you feel about yourself and, most important of all, how you feel about your audience. Good posture during your speech is imperative.

What is bad posture? You have seen it a million times. Some speakers come to the podium and turn it into a Lazy Boy™. They lean and slouch over the podium. They grasp the podium with their hands and never let go. They fiddle with their keys, their watches, or they put their hands in their pockets. They fidget and can't seem to stand still, or shift from one side to the other like a drunken sailor. Such posture will distract from the message. People will become distracted from what you are trying to say to them.

What is good speaking posture? Well, I believe a good speaking posture begins before you get to the speaking area. As a speaker, you should walk to the podium with a feeling of confidence. Your head should not be hanging low, or your hands clasped behind your back. You should face your audience with your feet slightly apart, your shoulders erect, and your back straight. I know, I know, it sounds like I am calling you to attention, as in the army. Well, you are right. That's the idea. This stance will quickly garner the attention of your audience, and cause them to sort of straighten up a bit, to turn their heads in your direction. Next, it will signal to your body and mind that you are prepared to speak. You are ready to enter the arena. You are prepared, confident, and ready to take them on. Good posture will do all of this for you.

Good posture will instantly connect you with your audience. They will feel that you are prepared and ready to deliver the message. Your erect shoulders will cause your head to look straight ahead into your audience. You will see their faces and they will see

BAD POSTURE

DO NOT ...

• Lean on the podium
  or lectern

• Put hands in your
  pockets or clasp them
  behind your back

• Rock on your feet or
  stand up like a statue

yours. This will give you your first full contact with your audience. This simple stance will quickly build rapport, and a sense that you are in charge and they should listen to what you have to say.

Should you remain in this position throughout your entire presentation? No. This is your opening move. It's like getting into the starting positions in a football game. Before the ball is snapped, all the players go into their starting positions. The stance signals that everyone is ready to go. Once the ball is snapped, everyone goes into action. It is the same for your speech. Once you get your opening words out—and those words should be designed to capture your audience's attention—then it's time to move around. Remember, this is just your game-opening stance. Afterwards, use your body to tell the story.

A lot of speakers stand behind the podium. In some situations, this is the best thing to do when delivering your presentation. The room may be set up in such a way that this is the only place for you to speak from. But if you can move around, I suggest you get away from the podium and engage your audience.

Moving away from the podium during the presentation will give you a sense of momentum. You can engage your entire body in the presentation. Moving away from the podium gives you the opportunity to make contact with the audience. You can move among them and get up close and personal. Don't stick to one area of the stage. Move about the stage and engage different areas of the room. Keep your notes with you.

Facial Expressions

Your facial expressions should be consistent with the message you're trying to convey. The expressions on your face should reflect your points and get your audience emotionally involved in the subject. This is not the time to play Mr. Spock from Star Trek. Mr. Spock was from the planet Vulcan. Vulcans had trained themselves to show no emotion. A solemn face, devoid of emotion or feeling, will only serve to distance you from your audience. You may come off as a stern lecturer rather than a friend. Remember, the key is to make a connection with the audience. A key to making that connection is with facial expressions that convey your message to the audience.

Your face has over 30 muscles. That's a lot. That means your face is capable of portraying a lot of emotion. Some say that the human face is capable of expressing 250,000 different looks. We have a great variety of expressions to choose from in order to express our feelings to an audience. The audience is looking at your facial expression in order to know how they should react to your message. If you're going to tell a funny story, then precede it with a smile. If your message is serious, then a more solemn look may be required. But for most of your speech you should maintain a warm, happy look on your face. A good thing to do is to smile before you start your speech. It takes about 15 muscles for your face to smile. Before you begin to speak, look out at your audience with a big smile. With a big warm smile on your face, you are already using up to 50 percent of that real estate between your ears. This will put your audience at ease and make them relax. So go ahead and smile.

EXERCISE #5
Practicing Facial Expressions

Perhaps you are thinking, "I can't control my facial expressions. I can't see what my face looks like while I am speaking." Well, yes you can. This is where your practice sessions come into play. While you are practicing, you can use one of several options. These options will help you become aware of what is happening to your face as you are speaking to an audience. You can choose to use one or all of them—it depends on how dedicated you are. I have listed these options in the order that I think will have the most impact on improving your facial expressions during your speech.

OPTION 1. The best thing to do is video tape yourself giving the speech. Many people taking my public speaking courses have found videotaping to be a very helpful tool for practicing the right facial expressions. You can see exactly how you form your face and how it looks to your audience. I highly recommend video taping your speech during a practice session. Afterward, review the tape, observe your facial expressions with an eye to applying as appropriate the suggestions you have read in this book. Think about your reactions to what you are seeing. Then put yourself in the audience and think how they will react to your facial expressions.

OPTION 2. The next best thing is to observe yourself in a mirror while you are giving your speech. This is a good way to observe yourself in real time. You can see your facial expressions as you are actually rehearsing your speech. You can practice certain expressions to perfection, pausing and reviewing at the moment you see a need for improvement. You can decide to add other expressions to strengthen your material. Or you may observe certain odd twitches and work on removing them. You can instantly remove expressions that do not fit the mood of the message you are conveying. A mirror is a great tool, and you can do this in your bathroom. It's a private place to practice and people in the house are more likely to leave you alone. I find the acoustics in the bathroom are great for speaking.

OPTION 3. Next, you can have someone observe you delivering your speech. The person who is helping you should be a good speaker. A good speaker will be able to give some excellent feedback on how to add or remove certain expressions. If you can afford it, get yourself a speech coach who will give you suggestions to help you dramatically improve your gestures. But in a pinch, a spouse or significant other may do. After all, they can act just like a miniature audience and give you their own feelings about what they are seeing and hearing. Having someone watch your face during a practice session can be very helpful in eliminating some of the more egregious problems with your facial expressions.

Your face can tell the audience a lot about you. Work very hard on making sure that your facial expressions match the message you are conveying to your audience. Use your facial expressions to get your audience on your side. You want to make them feel comfortable with you.

Gestures

As a speaking coach, one of the toughest questions I get from my clients is: What do I do with my hands? Many people are unsure of what to do with their hands while they're speaking. Your hands are not just appendages that need to be hidden. As you are learning, you should employ all visible body parts when giving a speech. This is especially true when it comes to the use of your arms and hands. A good speaker will employ gestures to keep the hands

> **FACIAL EXPRESSIONS**
>
> **DO NOT:**
>
> • Try to fake your expressions. Not only is it dishonest, but it will tend to turn off your audience and make them feel you cannot be trusted.
>
> • Frown or grimace throughout the whole presentation. This tends to make the audience uncomfortable.
>
> • Force facial expressions. Remember, the key is to be natural. Avoid the old "used car salesman" smile.

and arms occupied, and to help communicate the message to the audience.

We all do it, gesturing, some of us more than others. Yet the inexperienced speaker is often gripped by fear and becomes immobilized. Hands grip the podium and they never let go. Immobilized speakers are missing out on a valuable opportunity: Gestures reinforce your message and add emphasis to your words. Gestures can generally be divided into four distinct areas. The areas are descriptive, emphatic, suggestive, and prompting.

Descriptive gestures show action or indicate dimensions or locations. They can tell the audience how long, what shape, or which direction. When using descriptive gestures, you are visually describing the aspects of your speech that you wish the audience to see. You are giving a visual cue that supports what you are saying. Descriptive gestures emphasize the picture you are painting for your audience.

How can you use descriptive gestures in your speech? Perhaps when describing something that is large, you might extend your arms in an exaggerated manner, symbolizing something that is big or enormous. When you wish to convey that something is small, you can use thumb and forefinger gestures denoting smallness. It's very simple, and you do this all the time. All you have to do is think about it. But be careful, don't overdo it. When you are rehearsing your speech, practice a few descriptive gestures and stick to them.

Emphatic gestures are used to convey feelings and emotions to your audience. Emphatic gestures can be very powerful tools to use in bringing your audience into your world and making them feel the things you are feeling. You can use these gestures to arouse your audience to action. With these gestures you can convey your feelings to your audience.

How do you use emphatic gestures? They are the most common and varied gestures, and you can use them for the majority of your speaking time. One good gesture is to use your fingers when making a point. If you are going to make three separate points in your speech, you can start off by holding up the first finger to signify the first point. Then you go on and follow it through for the other points. At the end you can summarize the points by going through the fingers. Emphatic gestures can demonstrate strong emotion. You could raise a clenched fist over your head. Or you can point out at the audience, asking them to get involved.

A **suggestive gesture** is using your hands to bring in the audience. If I am presenting two alternatives to the audience, I will extend one arm for the first alternative, with palm extended out, then the next arm to demonstrate the second alternative. A shrug of the shoulders could signify bewilderment or amusement. Most of the time, I use my hands to emphasize the points I am trying to make with the audience.

Prompting gestures are also used to get your audience to follow your lead. If you want the audience to applaud, then you start applauding. If you want the audience to raise their hands, then you raise your hands. You are giving the audience an example of the behavior you wish to see.

I don't really want to give you too many suggestions when it comes to gesturing. I believe the best gestures come naturally. They are a part of your communication style. As I stated earlier, we all do it. What I want to do is to make you more aware of the fact that you should use gestures in your public speaking the same way as you would when speaking to an individual. This will take some work, but it is well worth it. Use your practice sessions to make sure you are using gestures purposely and naturally.

There is a danger in using emphatic gestures. Sometimes a speaker will overuse the gesture. Once he has a good gesture, he uses it again and again, and the gesture loses its impact and becomes more of a mannerism. Another problem is that the gesture can be too strong for the audience. Nikita Khrushchev was the Russian premier during the 1950s, a leader of one of the most powerful nations on earth. In a fit of impassioned drama during one of his speeches at the United Nations, he took off his shoe and pounded it on the lectern. This gesture made him look rather silly and uncouth. Hitler was famous for pounding his fist upon the podium like a madman. Well, he really was a madman. But I think you get the point. You don't want to come off that strong. If you are going to use strong, emphatic gestures, limit their use to maximize impact. Save your more powerful gestures for the end, when you may wish to emphasize the action you want the audience to take. But be careful, you do not want to alienate the audience by browbeating them. And please, keep your shoes on.

Another danger is that gestures can be misinterpreted. My son and I were riding a rollercoaster at a local amusement park a few years ago. As it happens, they snap photos of riders as they careen down the main rail. It's a great time to make a gesture and a funny face. Well, we both put up our two fingers, making peace signs. When we got off the coaster, the woman refused to give me my picture. She said I had made an obscene gesture. After further examination, it was clear that I had two fingers up and not one. What's the moral of the story? Sometimes your gestures may be misinterpreted. The key is to avoid gestures that could be interpreted in different ways.

Today, we live in a multicultural environment. The United States has really become a melting pot. In my neighborhood alone, there are people from all over the world. Why does this matter? It matters because some gestures have different connotations depending on your background. It may be good to run your speech past people from a different cultural background to see if you are violating any cultural taboos. If you are speaking in front of a group with a different cultural background, this could save you a lot of embarrassment. Remember, your goal is to have your message heard. You don't want to do anything that takes away from your message. The key to gestures is to keep it natural.

Eye Contact

The poets have it correct when they call the eyes the windows to our soul. In the western world, we like to look people in the eyes. We live in a world filled with misinformation, misdirection, and misunderstanding. We look to the eyes to tell us if a person is telling the truth. Can I believe in you, can I trust you? The eyes are the perfect instruments to garner the attention of your audience. Eye contact is essential to giving an effective presentation. It is very important that you master this particular tool, since it will create credibility with the audience.

Eye contact is also a gauge of how well your audience is receiving the message. By looking at the faces in the audience, you can tell if you are having the desired effect. Does your audience look confused, bewildered, or lost? Are they paying more attention to the lights in the ceiling than to what you have to say? Have you lost control of the situation? Are malcontents in the audience stealing the attention away from you and your message? Is your message getting through? You can only judge this if you are paying attention to the audience. You have to achieve eye contact.

Eye contact builds a connection with the individuals in your audience. While a presentation may be made to a handful, or to hundreds, your objective is still the same. You are trying to reach individuals with your message. Nothing is more powerful than to look at the individuals in your audience. Make them feel that they are part of your presentation. You want to let them know that you are talking to them, not talking at them. Eye contact is the perfect tool for establishing rapport with any audience. Many speakers do not use this technique, so right off the bat, you will be doing what the majority fail to do. The impact will be immediate. Learn this technique.

What is the key to establishing good eye contact? Actually, it begins before you give your speech. Good eye contact starts with good preparation. You should know your material like the back of your hand. You

USING NOTES DURING YOUR DELIVERY

- Lay notes on the lectern before your speech

- Look down at your notes at brief intervals

- Look at the keyword for your next point

- Finish the page you are on before moving to the next

- Pick up your notes when you are finished

should be able to say it in your sleep, while driving your car, or taking a shower. You should know exactly what you are trying to accomplish, and the information you are using to do so. It should be indelibly marked in your mind. If you follow the procedures I covered earlier in this book, your material will be hardwired into your mind and your objective is written in your heart. With this kind of familiarity you are ready to engage the audience with your eyes.

The most important tool you have at your disposal to help you establish good eye contact is your notes. If you have followed the suggestions I made to you earlier, your notes should consist of short, concise reminders to what you are going to say. Your notes act as signposts leading you through the journey of your discussion with the audience. Your notes become like a tether line that attaches astronauts to their spaceships. Astronauts who perform space walks are attached to the ship with a tether line. The line ensures that they don't float off by accident when they are doing their space-walks. Also, they can use the line to pull themselves back to the ship. The line gives the astronaut a sense of freedom. He is not worrying about floating off, and he knows there's a lifeline to bring him home. Your notes are like that lifeline when it comes to eye contact. Without having to worry about remembering each line or sentence, you have your notes to bring you back in line and keep you on the right path. The notes now give you the confidence to look out at the audience and engage them in the material.

How do you engage your audience with your eyes? Some speech professionals advocate scanning the audience like a radarscope, or following a particular pattern, like a robot. I don't recommend either of these approaches. They convey an unnatural and contrived feeling. The idea is to reach out to individuals in the audience. It is good to pick certain faces to look at from time to time. Make sure you pick out a friendly face (but not too friendly, or else you may break down and start laughing). Once you have found someone who is interested and following along, then just glance at this individual for about 20 seconds, no more. Pretend in your mind that you are just giving the speech to this one person. You and the individual are the only people in the room. But don't spend too much time. Now move on to other individuals. Make sure you are glancing at different areas of the room. Don't confine your glances to just those in a certain section.

As you look at the people in your audience, you will receive the most important thing that every speaker needs: feedback. This is real-time feedback. You should not only be looking at engaging your audience, you want to get a feeling for their receptiveness. Are they following along with you? Is your point having an impact? Can you see looks of wonder, or are you boring your audience? Make sure to look out at the back of the room. This will give you a good gauge as to whether you are speaking loud enough.

If you perceive that your information is not having the desired effect, don't be afraid to take another approach. I know, I know, you have this well-prepared speech that you spent hours working on and now I tell you to forget it. Not quite. What I am saying is to learn to be flexible and nimble on your feet. Maybe you change the pace, pitch, or volume of your voice. Or perhaps you can throw in a couple of questions to get things back on track. As a speaker, you have taken on a great responsibility. You should not abuse that responsibility by failing to listen to what your audience is telling you. Don't be afraid to vary somewhat off your beaten path as long as it gets you to your destination. So get out there and engage your audience with eye contact.

Vocal Presence

Modulation

Have you heard a good orchestra perform? It's a wonderful experience; all the various instruments harmoniously combine to produce a melody. The melody can make us happy or sad.

The most important instrument that you have as a speaker is your voice. All your research and preparation will be for naught if your material is delivered in a dry, monotone voice devoid of emotion. Many speakers mistakenly suppose that emotion is not important, that the audience will be dazzled by the mere presentation of dry facts and by their impeccable knowledge. But they are wrong.

As a speaker, it is your obligation to enliven your audience. Your objective should be to stir their emotions and give them a call to action. You must convince them of your sincerity and build a bridge of trust. A good part of this bridge is built on the tone of your voice. There are three key elements to the use of your voice in your presentations. The three elements are the three Ps: Power, Pace, and Pitch. We will discuss these in the following sections.

Power

A good speaker projects a sense of control and command of the space through the power of her voice. The key element in projecting power from the stage is the use of volume. If the volume of your voice is too low, then your message will not be heard. You will

USING A MICROPHONE PROPERLY

• Have microphone 4-6 inches from your mouth

• Keep microphone in front of you

• Speak up with your normal conversational voice

• Turn your head if you have to sneeze or cough

be considered weak and ineffective. After a few minutes, you will lose your audience. On the other hand, if the volume is too loud, it can irritate and turn off your audience very quickly. You will seem angry and impatient, like a lecturing schoolteacher. No one likes to be lectured. The key is to find a level of volume where you can be comfortably heard by people in the back of the room and not overwhelm those in the front of the room. There are three considerations to take into account when using volume.

Consider Your Environment

Are you speaking to an individual, small team, or a large group? Is it in an office or large auditorium? Are you going to be speaking with a microphone? You will have to adjust your volume to fit the circumstances of the environment. With a small group, lower your volume. If it is a large group, then increase the volume. My experience has been that most people do not speak loudly enough.

How can you determine if your speaking volume is adequate? If you arrive early and have a partner, you can have your partner go to the back of the room. Start speaking in a conversational tone. If your partner can hear you, then you are loud enough to be heard. Next, have the partner move to the front of the room to see if it's too loud. You can also judge during your presentation if your volume needs adjusting. Look at the faces in your audience. If people in the back seem to be leaning forward, straining to hear you, or not paying very close attention, these could be signs that you need to increase the volume. If you notice the people in the front whose faces seem unfriendly or distanced from you, these could be signals to lower the volume.

Remember, environmental conditions can change just like the weather. A microphone can go on the blink. Suddenly there is a disturbance, perhaps loud noises from a construction site. You may stop speaking, waiting for the disturbance to stop. But sometimes the noise may continue. Or the back of the room begins to fill up with last minute guests. That is the time to increase the volume. Actually, you can even ask the audience if you need to speak louder. Since they are interested in hearing you, they will be more than happy to help you out in this regard. Like the weatherman, you should be constantly checking the atmosphere for any changes and adjust your voice accordingly. The key is to make your message heard by all in attendance.

Consider Your Objective

One way to stimulate your audience to action is to increase your volume. Perhaps you have been explaining the importance of recycling. You have told the audience that recycling will save our planet and save us money. Now at the end, when you wish to rouse the audience to action, it's time to raise your volume. This will garner the attention of your audience and leave them with the lasting impression of the action you want them to take.

Consider Your Material

Volume can be used to emphasize certain points that you want your audience to remember. As we discussed earlier, the audience does not know which points are important unless you emphasize those points. One way to emphasize your point is to increase your volume when you are introducing your main points to the audience.

Lowering your volume is also an effective tool for gaining the attention of your audience. When your volume is lower, the audience has to pay more attention to what you are saying. It is especially appropriate if the point is something serious and you need to ensure the audience understands it. Or it may be appropriate when talking about something that is sad or painful and you need to convey that feeling to the audience. Again, the key here is that the audience still needs to be able to hear what it is you are saying.

Pace

Pace is the measure of how fast you are speaking. The strange thing about pacing is that all of us do it normally in our everyday speech. But for the inexperienced speaker, it's thrown aside very quickly. The new speaker spends so much time gathering the material and worrying about if he has delivered the message that he forgets about changing the speed of the spoken words. New speakers generally speak too fast, because they are nervous and want to get it over with. When you speak quickly, it's hard on the audience. You're taking them on a journey and they have to follow along. If you zoom by everything too fast, they will not be able to absorb all the information you are providing. At the end of the presentation they will be exhausted. If you move along too slow, you will lose your audience to boredom. The short human attention span will make them focus on other things besides you. Remember that the mind can absorb words faster than you can speak. A slow pace will cause that mind to wonder off in other directions. Also, you want to avoid speaking at such a measured pace that it never varies, and the audience is never given any sense of action or momentum.

Pace can be used to make your audience a part of the action. In movies, when the action begins to pick up, the music becomes louder and faster. The same is true when taking an aerobics class: The music starts off slow to get the circulation going, but then speeds up to stimulate the students to pick up the pace. You can capture the same effect by speeding up your words. You can create a sense of excitement or, bring the audience to a climax, just by the pacing of your words. Spicing up your speech with well-placed, accelerated pacing is bound to keep their attention.

Slowing down the pace brings some great advantages, too. Slow down when you come to particular points in your speech where you want to ensure that your audience retains the information. When you have brought your audience to a particular climax with the accelerated pacing, then it might be appropriate to slow down to make sure that the audience is getting the point. Slowing the pace can be utilized to dramatize a particular situation, to give it more weight. Remember, when reaching a main point, major argument, or climax in the delivery, slow down the pace.

Another way to slow things down, is silence. Silence can be a very powerful tool in the hands of a trained speaker. Most speakers don't use it because they don't know how to use it properly. Many consider silence as a show of weakness or not being in control. But if you learn to use it properly, silence can be just the opposite. When using that pregnant pause, make sure you are still engaging your audience with your eyes or else they may think you have zoned out on them. Ten to twenty seconds is long enough, you will have to judge depending upon the reaction of the audience.

Here are a few places where you can use silence:

The Climax – Just when you have made the most important point. This can be a great place to stop and just let your listeners absorb what they have just heard.

Important Point – You just stressed a point that you want to stick in the minds of the listeners.

Transitions – You are moving from one point to a new point. This will give your listeners a chance to rest their minds and prepare them for the next point.

Questions – This can be a great way of taking the sting out of a hostile question. Wait, don't rush to answer the question. Give yourself time to think about it.

Pacing is a powerful tool for public speaking. It is not difficult to master. Think about the material and your audience. Underline the main points; this is where you should slow down. For minor points or to convey a sense of action, speed up the words. Think of pacing as a rollercoaster ride. People ride rollercoasters because of the ups and downs. Make your pacing like the rollercoaster. Your speech should incorporate both highs and lows.

Pitch

No, we are not talking about baseball here. Imagine you are attending a concert. The curtain goes up, the musician begins to play. During the entire performance, the artist plays only one note. He plays it loud, he plays it soft, he plays it fast, he plays it slow.

Lacking the change in pitch, the music is not very appealing. As speakers, we have to adjust the pitch in our voices in order to make ourselves sound like a beautiful melody to the audience.

How do you get this change in pitch? You can increase the power to your voice at various points to change the pitch, or tone. Remember when you were a kid and your mother would call you? You could tell from the tone of her voice (the pitch) whether she was calling you for good or for bad. By varying the pitch, you can display a sense of emotion and connect with your audience. Working on pitch is a tough one. But it can be achieved through diligent practice and observing the styles of other good speakers.

Word Power

This is a good place to talk about what words you should use in your presentation. Painters use their paints and brush strokes to express their ideas and feelings. Speakers have the spoken word. Some books spend a lot a time teaching pronunciation and how to breathe and how you should roll your tongue. This book is not designed to teach you that. If you think you have a problem with speaking properly, I suggest you hire a speech coach who can provide you with the proper guidance. I am making an assumption that your language skills are adequate. With that being true, I have added what I consider a few guidelines that I believe will be of great assistance:

Word Warning:
- Avoid technical or shop jargon
- Avoid words that no one understands
- Avoid words you might have difficulty pronouncing

Another area that most speakers have trouble with is word whiskers. What are word whiskers? They are expressions we use as fillers. The commons ones are "you know", "and", "but", "also', 'well", "oh", "um" and "ah". These are what I call filler words. We use them to fill the air when either we don't know what to say next or we are making a transition from one point to the next. You need to eliminate these fillers from your speaking conversation. They are not necessary and can distract from the message.

There are two things that can be done to eliminate word whiskers. You can replace them with silence. Use the pausing technique mentioned earlier, and allow silence to fill the air. Second, when making a transition from one point to a new point, you can use transitional words or phrases.

Here is a list of transitional phrases and words that can be used when changing thoughts or moving from one main point to another: in addition, furthermore, moreover, likewise, similarly, hence, thus, for these reasons, therefore, in view of the foregoing, so then, however, on the other hand, on the contrary, formerly, heretofore, and so forth.

The above are excellent phrases and words that can be used to join ideas and sentences together. But there is a danger. Beware! Do not use the same words or phrases too often. That's why I gave you such a rich list to use. If you overuse the same word, your speech will begin to lapse into the boring territory. It's like putting too much salt on your French fries. It is best to use these phrases lightly. Also, have someone listen to your speech to make sure there are no phrases or words that you repeat over and over again.

Enthusiasm

In the Bible, Jesus said that love covers a whole lot of sins. In public speaking, enthusiasm will cover a whole lot of blunders. People are willing to forgive your mistakes if you seem sincere about what you are saying. An enthusiastic speaker shows that she cares about her audience and feels that what she is saying is important and worthy of effort. This is how you as a speaker should feel about every presentation you give. If you don't feel that way, then don't bother to give the presentation. Let's get real here. If you don't care about what you are presenting to the audience, why should they care about it? On top of that, you are abusing the most precious commodity we humans possess: our time. So if you don't have any enthusiasm, go out and get yourself a cup of it now.

How do I build up enthusiasm, you ask? It begins before you even reach the stage. You should have gathered enough information about your subject and audience so that you feel somewhat at ease about what you are going to present. You don't have to be the expert; the audience is not expecting expertise per se. You should be reasonably acquainted with the issues surrounding your chosen topic. If you have done the pre-work as covered in the preceding chapters, then you will have some basis for confidence, which is the foundation for enthusiasm.

To convey this sense of wonder to your audience, it should show on your face. Before you begin to speak, take a deep breath, and look out into the audience. Smile. Look at their faces. I mean, look right into their eyes. Let them know from your eye contact that you are prepared and ready. Then start off with a bang!

LESSONS LEARNED

Presentation Delivery Steps

1. **Proper attire. Dress for success**

2. **Good posture at podium**
   a. Stand up straight
   b. Face audience directly
   c. Engage the audience with movement

3. **Physical Presence**
   a. Facial expressions
      i. Warm smile
      ii. Match expressions to your message
      iii. Practice facial expressions
   b. Gestures
      i. Descriptive—Describing something
      ii. Emphatic—Emphasizing something
      iii. Suggestive—Normal gestures, leading gestures
   c. Eye contact
      i. Connect with the audience
      ii. Gauge if the audience is with you

4. **Vocal Presence**
   a. Power
   b. Pace
   c. Pitch
   d. Enthusiasm

POWER TECHNIQUES

Power Technique Introduction

This is the power techniques section of the book. It is designed to give you specialized knowledge of advance skills in making your presentation. I put this in a special section because I consider them to be essential to raising the bar of excellence.

There are numerous techniques I could have chosen to focus on. The techniques in this section are what I consider to be the most important. I have followed the premise I spoke about at the beginning, to give you the information that will help you give a quality presentation. I have trimmed away the minor points and left you with the essential elements necessary for having the most impact on your listeners. The information is right to the point, so that you can expend the least amount of time and energy learning and more time actually applying the techniques.

I chose to put these techniques in a special section of the book because they are deserving of their own mini sections. Unlike the pyramid model I have constructed for you to follow in preparing to deliver your speech, the techniques in this section are designed to stand alone. You don't have to follow them in any sort of arranged order to get the full impact. Actually, at various places in the book I have referred you to this section. You don't have to read the entire book before you begin to utilize the techniques mentioned here. The power technique section is a good place to turn to and get quick and fast advice on how to employ a technique in just a matter of minutes.

Being the organized person that I am, I could not help but arrange this section in an orderly fashion. I have listed the power techniques in order of importance. I list them in the order of which techniques I think will have the greatest impact with the audience. It starts with power technique No.1 and proceeds to No. 6 in order of importance. As I stated earlier, it is not necessary for you to follow any particular order. You can turn to this section and apply these tools at any juncture while reading this book.

Each of the techniques are short, easy reads. I have removed all excess verbage to give you the essence of what it is you need. I tell you how to put the application into your presentation. I feel that this will be one of the sections of the book that you will return to again and again to help you with polishing up your presentation. My suggestion is to look through this section often when preparing your speech. I am giving you the benefit of the experience of hundreds of speakers who have traveled down this path before.

I have a rule. I guess you did not expect to find another Reggie Rule here. This is a rule that applies not only to speaking, but to your life. It is the rule that experience is not always the best teacher. Sometimes someone else's experience can be a better teacher. This section of my book is filled with the experiences of others. Use it to the fullest to make your presentation the best it can be.

What Is In This Section

There are six power techniques:

Power Technique One: Use of Feedback – Every speaker needs to get honest and frank feedback on every presentation. Feedback is what helps you to improve. I will show you how to get feedback.

Power Technique Two: Use of Visual Aids – The greatest danger known to modern day presenters. It has coined its own phrase, "Death by PowerPoint". This technique will instruct you how to use visual aids appropriately.

Power Technique Three: Use of Stories – This can be a powerful tool in the hands of the right person. Stories can engage the audience. Follow the advice in this section.

Power Technique Four: Use of Humor – The second most dangerous tool for a speaker. If improperly employed, it could destroy the entire presentation. Learn to avoid the danger zones.

Power Technique Five: Handling Questions (Hostile) – Questions are a good way to engage your audience. But they can be dangerous if you don't know how to handle them when they turn hostile.

Power Technique Six: What to Do When Things Go Wrong – It's going to happen sooner or later. Your microphone goes dead, your visual aid fails, your dog eats your presentation. What do you do to keep the show on the road?

USE OF FEEDBACK

You have delivered your speech! Your hard work is done, right? Well, not quite. You still have a bit of work to do. You need to get feedback on how well you delivered your message. What if this is the only time you will ever deliver this particular speech? Minimally, it would be good to know how well you've applied your new skills to your presentation. Just because your topic or audience changes doesn't mean you can't apply feedback from one speaking opportunity to the next. Feedback will be invaluable for future presentations. Seek it out and use it.

How do you obtain feedback about your presentation? In talking about feedback, we'll move from the simple to the complex. There are many sources to pursue. It depends on how much you really care about improving your speaking ability. The more sophisticated the feedback mechanism employed, the more improvement realized. Improving a few things with every speech will have a dramatic impact on your future presentations.

The only bad feedback is the feedback you don't receive. Don't take negative feedback personally. That may be hard to do since it often seems directed at you. Even though I have been getting feedback on my presentations for almost twenty years, I still cringe a little even today. But remember, you are using this information to become a better speaker. The biggest room in the world is the room for self improvement. There are no perfect speakers. Each speaker has weaknesses and strengths. It is good to know what are your strong and weak points. Early on, I told you that the best speakers are the best listeners. This is a great place for you to listen and learn.

During the Presentation. You've already received feedback in various forms before you gave your presentation. But once your presentation begins, a new and valuable source of feedback is literally staring you in the face. It's the very people for whom your presentation has been crafted. Are they buying? This feedback should never be ignored.

What is the audience doing while you are speaking? What do their faces look like? Are they laughing at your jokes? Are they absorbed in what you are saying? Do they look bored, or perplexed? Looking at your audience will give you instant feedback. The very best speakers will take note of this and change the presentation immediately to grab the audience's attention. Pay very close attention to your audience when you make the closing line. Do they get it? Do they seem ready to take the action you are proposing?

After the Presentation. When you have made your closing remarks and your presentation is done, you can garner quick feedback in a more relaxed way. You can ask some of the listeners if they enjoyed the presentation. What did they like about the presentation? Ask some questions based on the presentation to see if they remember any of the main points. Listen to the words they use to describe your speaking ability. Do they seem excited about the topic? Are they more informed than they were before you began speaking? How do they feel about you, if you are a stranger? A sure sign that you were a hit is that, when the presentation is over, people wish to discuss some of the points you mentioned during your presentation. If they were bored or turned off, they would not ask for any more information about the subject.

There is a down side to the more informal, relaxed feedback session. The people who approach you may be only the ones who liked what they heard, or they may just be the extroverts in the group. Individuals who could provide more balanced input may be heading out the door before you can meet them. After one speech, I came off the stage and one person monopolized so much of my time that I did not get to speak to anyone else in the room. Also, people are reluctant to say anything bad about your presentation in such a setting. They don't want to embarrass you, or come off as a know-it-all or malcontent. Someone may wish to give you some ideas on how to improve but may be afraid about how it will be received.

The next step up from informal feedback is to have the entire audience rate you. You can place survey cards on their chairs. List some of the general things you would want to know. Ask them to rate you from 1 to 5, 5 being great. You could ask questions like did the speaker clearly articulate the message? Did the speaker explain things clearly? Leave room on the card for them to write in their own comments. When you collect them you can total up your scores in specific areas and have a very scientific method for rating the effectiveness of your presentation skills. When reading the comments section, you should look for trends. If 20 people say that you talk too loud, you should lower your voice. The trends can give you a good measure of how the audience is receiving your message. This is the ultimate in audience participation.

There are some drawbacks to allowing the entire audience to rate you. You have to sit down and think about what kind of questions you wish to ask the audience. This is not as easy as it sounds. Since your audience in general may know little about proper speaking techniques, there may be things they would overlook. The ratings may not give you a specific area you need to work on. Also, there are logistical complications. You have to make sure the forms are produced, distributed and collected. And then you have to tally the results and read all the comments. This can be very time consuming. A variation of the response card is that you could get their response via email. Unfortunately, because people are wary of junk email, you may not get as many responses as you would from a response card at your presentation. This is yet another way to know how your audience reacts to you and whether they are getting the message.

Here's one that's sort of quirky, but it has been tried and proven effective. I call it the bathroom poll. If you are the last speaker, or speak just before a break, run off the stage and head to the restroom. Lock yourself in one of the stalls. Then wait and listen. There's a good chance that those who come in the restroom to refresh themselves will talk about your speech and how they liked it. It's an interesting way to poll your audience. This technique actually works. My wife had this experience after one of my speeches. The women were in the bathroom raving about my speech, not knowing that my wife was among them.

A specific way to get great feedback is to have someone who is a skilled speaker observe your presentation. This can be invaluable for improving your presentation skills. A good speaker will be able to give an effective and balanced evaluation. This person can bring things to your attention that your audience overlooked in the presentation. A good evaluator can offer you specific suggestions on how to improve certain aspects of your presentation.

Be careful: Not every good speaker is a good evaluator. Some people have a natural ability to speak but may lack good evaluation skills. A good evaluator needs to be a keen observer. The evaluator is listening to the speech, looking at your gestures, examining the audience for reaction, hearing the words, and doing a thousand comparisons in their heads. While all this is going on, the evaluator cannot get too caught up in the content of what you are saying, but needs to be ever-attentive to how you are saying it. Most individuals don't have the training to perform this task. But there are a few things you can do.

If the person you are using is new and has never done this before, you should give them some advice to help them through the process. Here are a few tips you can mention to your evaluators:

1. This is not a critique. The idea is to look for areas for improvement
2. Take written notes during the presentation. Refer back to the notes

3. Describe the strong points of the speech. What was good about it?
4. Describe the weak points, and how they may be improved
5. You don't have to make a comment in every section of the evaluation form
6. Concentrate on one or two areas for improvement
7. Use the sandwich method of evaluation
   a. Tell the speaker what was good about the presentation
   b. Tell the speaker what areas needs to be improved
   c. End the evaluation on a positive note

This is where you might bring in a speech coach. I spend a lot of my coaching time working with speakers in the real world. I examine and teach right up at the front line where the hard lessons are learned and are most apparent to clients. A coach will be intimately familiar with all of your quirks, and can focus on the areas you are looking to improve. Professional coaches are trained to filter out all the distractions and concentrate totally on you. A coach brings to the table years of experience and wisdom in how to help you overcome your hurdles. And the coach will be with you through it all to give you guidance and confidence. A speech coach can be a good option at this time.

If you don't want to spend the money, there's a way to get a trained evaluator to evaluate you for free. You could find out if any of your co-workers is a Toastmaster member. Toastmasters is an international speaking club. It teaches speaking and effective evaluation skills. Make sure the person is an active member and meet with the person to discuss your objectives and the specific points you want them to observe. This can be almost as good as having a paid coach. Being evaluated by a member of Toastmasters can be a free alternative to hiring a professional speech coach.

Another way is to assign the evaluation to a few close acquaintances. You can write up an evaluation form like the one mentioned earlier. This form would be more detail oriented toward the precise presentation skills you are working to perfect. You would bring these individuals together before you speak to brief them on how to do the evaluation and on your expectations and objectives. Make sure they understand what you are expecting of them. After the speech, it would be good to meet with them as a group. Have them give you the evaluation together. Now you will have a group consensus evaluation, which would be far more valuable to you than one individual. I suggest you use a minimum of three people for this particular approach.

Now that you have gathered the evaluation material together, what do you do with it? Good question. Many of my students have applied the techniques mentioned above, but failed to do the most important thing after they have gathered the evaluation information. They look it over, but they don't look at the information with an eye toward how they can sharpen their presentation skills. Most are so glad it's over with that they don't want to think about it anymore. They shove the papers in a draw and start working on the next thing. Please don't do that.

You need to pull out those papers and examine them very closely. I tend to go backwards. I like to read what I consider the areas for improvement first. I am a little more thick skinned than most, and have been doing this for a long time. First, compile all the good and positive comments that have been made about your presentation. Put them down on a sheet of paper. You don't need to write it word for word, but just capture the essence of the comment. Did you tell an interesting story and they all liked it? Write down "good storyteller." You get the picture.

Look over all of the positive comments you received. Now pat yourself on the back. You've come a long way. From these comments you will confirm your strengths. Unlike other speaking training programs, I believe that a speaker should play up his strengths and not worry too much about eliminating a weakness. How so? If everyone says that you are great at telling a story, then go with that. Make sure to include stories in all your presentations. You see, that's a strength that will grab your audience's attention. Make a list of these things and hold on to it, because the more you speak, the longer this list will become. That sounds strange, but here's how it works. As you become more comfortable with your strengths, you don't spend as much time working to perfect them, so you can move on to develop other areas you would like to make stronger. This gives you a firm foundation upon which to build your skills. You now have a working base that can sustain you through whatever presentation you give.

For me, I have a knack for giving wonderful illustrations. People are always asking me where I get my illustrations. Many cannot believe it when I say that I make them up myself. They just seem to come naturally. I can see a situation and think of a good comparison or illustration to fit the subject. Since I understand that this is a strong point, I don't spend a lot time working to perfect it. I expend my preparation energies in other areas that may need some improvement.

Let's talk about improvement. Now you can look through the comments and scores looking for areas of improvement. If one person says you were too loud, and it's one comment out of 35, don't take it too seriously. But if 34 people say you are too loud, then you have an area for improvement. Write down these particular points on a sheet of paper. Now you have a list of things that may need improvement. Look them over and see if there are places that you can apply an immediate fix. If many felt that your voice was low, then you need to increase the volume. There may be some things that will take a while to fix. Being from the Deep South, I sometimes mispronounce words with the best of them. I have been in the speaking biz for 20 years and I still get called on it.

When I first started speaking, I was a minister. Some found that when I spoke outside the congregation on secular matters, I sounded more like I was preaching. Well, nobody wants to be preached to in a corporate presentation. I had to work on that. But in time, I was able to change that perception through the use of the techniques I espouse in this book. It did not happen overnight, I worked for several years to overcome this problem.

I don't want you to get caught up with viewing less-than-flattering comments as something negative. How are you going to improve as a speaker if everyone tells you that you are wonderful, inspiring, and the greatest speaker they ever heard? All those things may be true, but speaking is an art. A true artist is never satisfied with the last work. The artist is looking to make the next piece of art bigger and better than the last. That same motivation will move you forward. So don't get bogged down in feeling bad for yourself if you receive some negative comments. Write them down and work on them. They will help you advance as a speaker.

Also, don't get caught up with trying to work on too many things at the same time. If your feedback suggests that your gestures, body language, and voice volume were not good, start by singling out one of those things to work on. It is better to work to improve one thing and get that one thing right than to spread yourself across several things and do all of them poorly. Just focus on the one you would most like to work on. In this book I have listed the essential techniques and how to use them. These are what you should concentrate on.

The message in feedback is to not beat yourself up. Recognize that we all have strengths and weaknesses. Some of these things make take a long time to work on. When I mentioned my corporate presentation sounding somewhat preachy, I should mention that I was very sensitive about that criticism. I was quick to dismiss it when it came up. I would say that they were misunderstanding my enthusiasm and energy and confusing it with being preachy. But after awhile, I recognized that it does not matter what *I thought* about my style. The only thing that really matters is *how the audience responds* to me. And with that, I vowed to change my image. I was able to do that.

As a speaker you will always be changing how you present your material. That is one of the most exciting aspects of speaking before an audience. There's immediate response and feedback that you can fold back into the improvement loop. By incorporating these things, you become better and better. I once spoke at an event, and someone commented that I sounded more relaxed, calm, and controlled than the last time they had seen me. This same person had always admired my speaking ability, yet he could see that I was working on improving my abilities.

I am putting the challenge before you today. Most books, seminars, and tapes on public speaking give scant coverage to the concept of receiving feedback. They give you their method for successful speaking and say, "Apply this and it will work." Well, it does not always turn out that way. Some techniques will work better for you than others. And you will not find that out if you do not seek the feedback of others. You need to have an intimate understanding of your capabilities, because this will give you the confidence you need to move ahead.

Getting feedback is one of the most important aspects of public speaking. I said in the beginning and throughout this publication that the best speakers are the best listeners. A good speaker has to listen to the audience. You have to understand their concerns, cares, and needs. It is your job to meet those needs, to incorporate them into your presentation. As a speaker you have a sacred obligation to respect those who have come to listen to your message. And the ultimate show of respect is to listen to your audience.

To help with evaluating yourself for continuous improvement, I have included on the following page a feedback form that you can use in all your presentations. It can be used to evaluate all the presentation skills and techniques you have been learning throughout the course of this book.

In this presentation, the speaker is working on the following skill sets. You are to rate the skill on the following chart. Circle your response: 1 – Needs improvement, 2 – Fair, 3 – Good, 4 – Excellent, and 5 – Outstanding. Please write any comments you have in the comment section.

		comments
Appearance	1 2 3 4 5	
Posture	1 2 3 4 5	
Gestures	1 2 3 4 5	
Eye Contact	1 2 3 4 5	
Organization	1 2 3 4 5	
Voice Volume	1 2 3 4 5	
Speaking Rate	1 2 3 4 5	
Voice Pitch	1 2 3 4 5	
Articulation	1 2 3 4 5	
Preparation	1 2 3 4 5	

Comments:

USE OF VISUAL AIDS

One of the best things that a speaker can use in a presentation is visual aids. One of the worst things a speaker can use in a presentation is visual aids. Sounds contradictory, and it is. Beware: Visual aids are like a two-edged sword. On one hand, they help to reinforce what you are telling your audience. Remember the chart showing how we learn? We tend to learn more from what we see than what we hear. I guess that's why there are no best-selling aerobic books on the New York Times list. When the visual is combined with the verbal, audience retention rates increase fourfold. Also, the visual aid is often something that can be left with the members of the audience to help them remember what you said.

But there is a bad side to visual aids. They can become a crutch for individuals who are not willing to prepare themselves properly. Many speakers crunch all their information onto a few slides, and then read them to the audience. The speaker is treating the audience like children, not like thinking, feeling, sensing adults. And on many occasions, speakers tend to overuse visual aids, using too many slides or piling together too much information on one particular medium. There are many pitfalls that are involved in the use of visual aids.

This power technique section is designed to give you some crucial information on how to take advantage—and avoid the pitfalls—of visual aids. It will give you the tips you need to know and provide you with a handy checklist you can use when employing visual aids. These techniques have been tried and proven. They are battle tested and ready for you to use freely. To make the best use of this power technique, I will be asking you a series of questions to determine how you should best deploy this particular speaking technique.

Do you need a visual aid? A strange question to ask, but it is often something people don't give a lot of thought. Is it really necessary to use a visual aid? A few years ago, when the visual aid technology was just beginning to take off, I would have answered a definite "yes." That's because most audiences were unfamiliar with all the new presentation technology. The use of multimedia presentations was fresh, and very few people knew how to utilize the medium, so most presentations were devoid of the use of technology. This was a good way for a person to show off their technical prowess and to totally mesmerize the audience. But things have changed now: Almost any kid with a computer can whip out a multimedia presentation in no time. Most of the tools are readily available. So what was once uncommon has become something we are all used to seeing. Having visual aids in itself will not set you apart from the crowd.

In today's corporate boardrooms a visual presentation is considered par for the course. That's why you may want to consider not using visual aids at all. There are some definite advantages to foregoing the use of visual aids. One thing is that you don't have to read over this power technique section of my book. You can concentrate all your energy and time on working on other aspects of your presentation skills. It's one less thing you have to worry about. As we will discuss later in this section, there are many things that should be considered when using a visual aid.

Actually not having visual aids could make you stand out among others in the business world today. Once I had to deliver a technical presentation to a large audience of technical managers. I knew they were used to getting the same old, tired slide presentation with facts and drawings ad nauseum. I knew that the others who were going before me would bore them to death with their PowerPoint presentations. So I decided to ditch the visuals and speak directly to them. The effect was powerful because it was unexpected, and a welcome retreat from all that went on before me. I set a bit of a trend for a while in those corporate meetings. You might wish to consider ditching the visual aids.

There are also great advantages to having visual aids. Let's face it, I don't care how brilliant you are as a speaker, no one will be able to remember every word you said. One way to ensure that the points you wish to make to the audience remain tangible and recorded is to have a visual aid. If you are presenting very technical information to an audience not familiar with what you are speaking about, it is almost a given that you should have a visual presentation. Also, the visual representation can act as cue for you to remember your lines and help you present the material. This can take some of the pressure off you to remember what you are supposed to say.

VISUAL AID	ADVANTAGE	DISADVANTAGE
PowerPoint Slides	Looks Professional, Good for large audiences	Distracts audience, prone to technical difficulties
Overhead Projector	Easy, Quick to set up	Same
Posters	Fast, Easy to make changes	Too small for large groups
Handouts	Helps audience retain information.	Distracts audience during presentation
Objects	Good when demonstrating a device.	Object demonstration can suffer glitch.
Flipcharts	Excellent for generation of audience participation.	Can be difficult to see. Handwriting can be illegible.
Whiteboards	Good for making drawings and showing connections	Not suitable for large audiences
Chalkboards	Same	Same

USE OF VISUAL AIDS

How do you handle visual aids? Here are three simple rules for use of visual aids:

1. Speak to your audience. Remember to keep eye contact. Do not start talking to the visual. Keep your eyes focused on the audience; refer back to the visual when appropriate.

2. Visuals should be visible. Make sure that everyone can see the visual you are using. Check to ensure that the room is setup in such a way as to allow the audience to view the visual.

3. Show visuals at the right time. Make sure that you introduce and comment on the visual aid at the appropriate time. Timing is everything when showing a visual aid. You want to show the visual when you are speaking about the subject the visual addresses.

Also, what is great about a visual aid is that it can be put into the hands of the audience. They can take it away and remember what you said. It can be given to the people who were not able to attend the presentation. A visual aid can be helpful in organizing your material.

What is an appropriate visual aid? If you have decided that this medium will enhance your presentation, the next thing is to choose a visual aid which is best suited for your audience. Yes, not for you, for the audience. I have included a visual aid matrix to assist you in making that decision. The choice of medium should be driven by your environment and the objective you wish to accomplish. Look at the matrix, examine the advantages and disadvantages. Then choose the medium which will enhance your presentation.

Whatever visual aid you choose, it should meet the following criteria to ensure that it is the right tool for the right audience:

Flawless. Make sure that the visual aid has no errors. Check your spelling and grammar to make sure you are using the proper terms, and if you are using a diagram, make sure it is accurate. There is no faster way to lose credibility than to have a flaw in your visual aid.

Easy to use. Make sure that you keep the visuals simple. Don't go overboard on the complexity. The more complex the visual aid, the more chance there is that something will go wrong. I can give you more than a few stories of how I planned to use an elaborate visual, but did not really know how to handle the technological glitches. It would have been better if I had not had a visual aid at all. Make sure that you can handle the visual aid easily.

Relevant. The visual should be connected to what you are talking about. The visual should enhance what you are talking about. Do not choose a visual that overwhelms your subject. The visual should work along with your message.

Since the majority of presentations are centered on the use of PowerPoint, here are a few tips:

1. Check your equipment before making the presentation. Ensure that the facilitator is using the correct equipment and software.
2. Do not put too much information on one slide. It will be too distracting. Generally I would not use more than six lines on a page, fewer if you can get away with it.
3. "Spell check" your slides before your presentation. Make sure the slides are all the same font.
4. Be prepared for a disaster, power outage, machine failure, etc. I have a section devoted to handling those occasional technical glitches.
5. Do not get too cutesy. Don't add a lot of noises, music, and cute animation unless you really know what you are doing and know your audience well.
6. Don't overdo it. Do not use too many slides. Consolidate, revise, and try to use the minimum slides needed to express your points.

If visual aids are used correctly, they can add a lot to your presentation. The tips mentioned in this section should help you use your visual aid to enhance the message you are trying to get across to the audience.

USE OF VISUAL AIDS

USE OF STORIES

Everyone loves to hear a story. It is universal to all cultures. Before humans learned how to write, we were telling stories to one another. Stories are interwoven into our society. They help to explain, to teach, and to make us feel good about ourselves and the world around us. We used to swap stories in the dark around the campfire and now we sit in darkened theaters to watch them. We all like to hear a good story.

Telling stories can be an excellent technique to use in your presentation. Stories have a way of moving people. Stories can take a complex situation and make it simple. The greatest thing a speaker can do is to make her message digestible and easy to understand. Telling a story can go a long way in that direction.

How do you tell a story? First you have to get one. I think the best stories come from your own life. They are the kind of stories that you know best. You should have no problems; after all, it's your life we are talking about. This is a good time to review the biography you filled out in Level II. Hey, did you know you would be getting so much mileage out of that bio? I am sure if you look back on your many experiences, there are many stories you can recall.

Of course, you can always tell someone else's story. This could be a story about something that happened to someone else. Or you could tell a story that someone else has told you. Telling other people's stories can be a good thing. Perhaps you have already seen how the story works and the effect it can have on an audience. There can be drawbacks to using someone else's story. You might find that your audience has heard the story before. Maybe they have even heard the story told better than you tell it. That's the worst thing that can happen. Or the story has a particular punch line, which now the audience will already be too familiar with.

Whatever the origins for the story, there is a methodology that can be applied to help you use the story telling technique. These are easy steps to follow. Here are three secrets for using stories in your presentation:

Relevant. I don't care how good the story is, it must be relevant to the subject you are speaking about. The audience should be able to quickly make a clear connection between the story and the main theme. The story should be tightly woven within the fabric of the presentation.

Well Rehearsed. Telling a story requires more practice than your regular speech. The story should be told without the use of notes. You need to look at the audience and engage them into the story. This cannot be done if you read to the audience. Now there is an exception, if the story is short and perhaps you are reading it for effect. But you should be reading it in such a way as to not seem like you are reading it. Refer to the end of the Delivery section to refresh your memory on how this should be done.

Impact. The best stories should engage the emotions of the audience. People like to be transported to a new place by a good story.

USE OF STORIES

USE OF HUMOR

Humor is one of the best techniques for making an instant connection with the audience. Everyone likes to laugh. And everyone likes a person who can make them laugh. They want to be around you, they are paying attention to every word you are saying. Humor is an excellent bridge and a powerful attention grabber. That's why I listed it as one of the great ways to introduce yourself to the audience.

The problem with humor is that it has to be done almost flawlessly. In your speech you can make a few errors and people will tend to forgive you for it. You may mispronounce a word or two, or even turn a sentence around. But when employing humor, the listeners will not grant you the same leeway. A mispronounced word or a sentence turned the wrong way can automatically change the entire thrust of the humor, rendering it remarkably unfunny. Humor has to be executed flawlessly in order for it to work. Don't worry, this section will help you.

Another drawback that I mentioned earlier is that humor can be dangerous. What may be funny to your social circle may not be appropriate to tell to a larger audience. As I stated, the range of inappropriate humor has expanded exponentially over the last few years with the inclusion of more diverse cultures into our own. Cultural experiences differ greatly, and some may not get the humor of the joke you have just told.

Once I was teaching a very diverse class. Half the class was made up of Asian students. A joke was told about baseball. Since most of them were unfamiliar with the game, few of them could really understand the humor that was employed.

But I don't want to scare you off from using humor. I just want to make sure you understand the potential pitfalls of using it. I believe that all presentations should contain a bit of humor. After all, it's an obvious way to make sure that your presentation is not boring. The wonderful thing about humor is that you can combine storytelling and humor together. There's nothing as powerful as a short, funny story. It's not my place here to turn you into a standup comedian. But you can learn to incorporate humor into your presentation to better connect with your audience.

Sources of Humor

Where did he get those funny stories? Today, there is a wealth of sources for humor. Fortunately, the Great Wasteland (TV) can provide a bounty of humorous stories and jokes. In fact, there is an entire channel devoted to comedy. While not all the jokes may be suitable for your audiences, it is a good place to observe how humor works. I will address that in just a few moments. Your video store is also a great place to look for humor. However, I have to admit that I am a sentimentalist when it comes to humor. I feel that much of today's humor is rough, crude, and lacking ingenuity. The masters of subtle humor are the Marx Brothers. I would recommend if you are truly interested in the employment of subtle humor, get yourself some popcorn and watch a few Marx Brothers films. The great thing is that you can sit down with the whole family for this phase of your preparation.

Another source for humor is other people. Let's face it: There are some bright, funny people out there. We can listen to them, or even buy their books. The drawback here is that if you have heard

USE OF HUMOR

it that means there is a chance that many others have heard it too. That's why I like the Marx Brothers: They wrote all their stuff in the 1940s and most people don't watch them today. So you can look for old humor. Abraham Lincoln is another source to borrow humorous stories from. I have used his stories before, and no one seems to have heard them. Make sure that if you are using someone else's story, you attribute it to the person.

The best source for humor is the person who is reading this book at the moment. Yes, that's you. Oh, you are thinking that you are not a funny person. Well, that's not true. No doubt if you look back on your biography, there are hundreds of things that have happened to you that seem quite humorous. Maybe at the time it was not funny, but in hindsight, it now appears funny.

I know this is true, because I had a woman in one of my classes who was very uptight and had a hard time telling a joke. But when she spoke about her life in India, it was really funny. She did not realize that her experiences could be so entertaining.

Also, you can exaggerate your experiences for comic relief. This is a great way to bring humor to your audience. You can take an ordinary circumstance, and exaggerate it to make it funny. The master of this is Bill Cosby. If you can, try to watch some of his old shows where he tells a story. He is great. But you don't have to be on that level to do it well. Here's an example:

> *When I was registering for college, we did not have computers to assist in registration. We had to chisel our names on stone tablets. I did not have to read the philosophy of Aristotle, since he was still teaching classes when I was a freshman.*

That's an example of exaggeration. Of course there is no need to explain it since the audience already knows that you are exaggerating the facts to make a point. This is a powerful technique to use. The great thing about exaggerating is that you don't have to worry about anyone telling the story before you, because it belongs to you. And as with every good story, it will tend to get funnier and better as you use it on different audiences.

But it is simply not enough to tell a good story. Humor is also in how the tale is told. Humor is all about timing. Two people can tell the same exact story, one is funny and the other is not. Timing makes a big difference.

In humor, it's all about the delivery. Don't start laughing at your own jokes. Maintain a firm smile and a good posture. Let the humorous story tell itself, don't force or rush it. Allow time for the audience to absorb the humor. The best place to learn this is by watching others who do it well. I don't recommend joke books, or books on humor. Most of them are not very good.

Here are some hints to help you.

1. Test out the joke or humorous story on your family and friends, preferably people whose sense of humor you trust.
2. Look for others with diverse backgrounds and tell it in a small group. Get their reactions.
3. If the joke or humorous story bombs, find out why.
4. Keep it simple. The more complex the joke, the less funny it will be.

USE OF HUMOR

USE OF QUESTIONS

Nothing is more fraught with danger than the use of questions during a speech. I have seen many a good speech go down the drain because the speaker did not know how to answer questions correctly. The danger with questions is that, throughout your entire speech, you have complete control of the entire process. You have done the research, the preparation, and maybe even made a flawless delivery. But when the floor is thrown open to questions, you are no longer in control. Now someone else can grab control of the room. And unless you know what to do, you may find your presentation spiraling out of control.

Earlier in the book, I discussed some basics about how to handle questions when making a presentation. What I am presenting here are some advanced techniques you can employ to help you keep control of the situation. I divided these into what I call the Curious and the Hostile questioners.

Curious Questions. These are legitimate questions from people who really want to understand the information you have just given. They might have missed something in the presentation, or maybe there was information they feel you should have covered.

Hostile Questions. Sometimes these are legitimate questions, but most of the time they are not. They come from people who may be hostile to what you are saying. Their agenda may be to sabotage your presentation by peppering you with a lot of questions that are outside the scope of the presentation. It is easy to recognize them: Arms are folded across the chest as they lean back in the chair, and during your presentation they may have a scowl on their faces. Often they have already made up their minds before you even come on the stage. Beware. You can't just ignore them. You have to know how to deal with them.

Here are the guidelines for answering questions.

If you don't know the answer to a question or are not sure of the answer, just say that. I know it's supposed to be heresy to say you don't know something. But it is important to maintain your authenticity. Nothing can trash authenticity more than to be caught in a lie or giving information that is not factual. It is perfectly okay to say you don't know. Now, here's the next step. Tell the person that you don't know, but you will find out and get back to him. It is very important that you get back to the person with the answer. Lying to him is not the way to gain trust.

Repeat the question for clarity. It is good to repeat back the question to the person who asked it. This will accomplish two things. One, if it's a large audience, there's a chance that some people may not have heard the question. Second, you want to make sure that you are answering the right question. You can do it more subtly by just including the question within the answer.

Keep the answer simple. Try to avoid long answers. Answer the question as succinctly as possible. Try not to go off on a different tangent with the question.

Acknowledge the questioner. Make sure you acknowledge the person who asked the question. Look at her to make sure you have answered the question. Check to make sure that it has been answered to her satisfaction. For this you can just look at their faces and gestures to see if the answer suited them.

How to Solicit Questions

Every now and then, you will have that group of people who may be a little shy about asking questions. Here are a few tips to get your audience involved:

1. Ask a question to the audience in general
2. Ask a question to an individual in the audience
3. Select someone beforehand to ask you a question

Sometimes you may have to engage in verbal self-defense. An individual or perhaps even a small group may be trying to sabotage the presentation. There may be many reasons for this, but the point is that you need to get yourself back in control. Here are some suggestions for handling hostile questions.

1. Clarify. Make sure your point is clear to the audience.
2. Relax. Don't tense up, or show frustration. Remain calm and cool.
3. Find common ground. Point out your similarities.
4. Be honest. Always tell the truth, never mislead.
5. Reverse it. Put the person on the spot. Turn the question around.
6. Quit. Sometimes it's best to fold 'em. Just end the conversation.

Here are a few phrases which can help you out of a hostile situation:

1. Let's take up that question after the session.
2. That's a great question. How about if we take this discussion offline.
3. We need to move on so we can get a few other questions answered.
4. I can understand how you feel. But we have to move on now.
5. We're sort of limited in time for questions. How about if we discuss that later.
6. I've noted your concerns. Now let's move on to someone else.

WHEN THINGS GO WRONG

The one thing that you can count on is that things are bound to go wrong at some point in your presentation. You are bound to encounter snafus, glitches, blunders, mistakes, and just plain old misfortune. Get over it. It's just the nature of the beast. There are things that are not in your control that can get out of control. The crux of the matter is not what happens, but how you respond to what has happened, that will make all the difference in the world. You can take a bad situation and make it better. If you get lemons, then squeeze them and make lemonade.

Since I speak a lot, I have experienced them all. I feel qualified to give you some pointers about how to deal with problems when they occur. I have created this "survivor package" to help you along the way.

The first key to surviving when things go wrong is to be prepared for the disaster. Old Ben Franklin had it right: An ounce of prevention is worth a pound of cure. Always have a plan B. If you are using Power Point slides or an overhead projector for your presentation, recognize that these gadgets can go out on you. Therefore, bring along handouts of your presentation. If the gadget goes, you can still deliver your information to the audience.

Don't get too caught up in what has gone wrong. Keep your focus on the audience, not on the mishap. Keep on working. If the microphone loses power, or does not work properly, cast off the microphone, move away from the podium and go down to the audience level and engage them there. Take your notes with you—they won't mind. Just make sure that they feel you are still in command of the room.

Sometimes you may be interrupted by a disturbance outside of the room. Have the doors shut or windows closed. If the noise continues, then speak up louder. Don't try to go out and rectify the situation yourself. The host can take care of that for you. Sometimes you won't be able to lose the distraction, so you may have to juice up your presentation a notch to keep the audience focused on you.

It is good to have a few one-line expressions to use for when things go wrong. Once when the lights started blinking during a presentation I was making, I said, "Now that's what I call a special effect." Have a few one-liners you can use to put your audience at ease. I don't want to give you a list of them; you can come up with those on your own. Besides, I don't want you stealing my thunder!

Of course the ultimate "bad thing" is that you forget what you are going to say. This is probably the most embarrassing and nerve-wracking thing that can happen to a speaker. Suddenly your mind goes blank and there are 100 pairs of eyes drilling into you, waiting for that next sentence. What do you do now?

First, go back to your notes. Look at them and find your place. It's okay. You can even make a joke about how you lost your place and need to get yourself oriented. No matter how good you get, you should always have your notes handy. You can even ask the audience to help you out. "Now what was that I was saying"? Don't worry, someone will tell you where you were.

What if there is a real problem—an earthquake, a fire, a flood, a medical emergency? I think this would be a good time to stop the presentation. Give the floor to the appropriate person who can give assistance. Make yourself helpful and work with the audience to assure that everyone is safe and secure.

The key to overcoming blunders, glitches, and mistakes is this: Do not panic. If you feel like sweating, sweat on the inside, not the outside. Stay in control of the situation. Use humor if you can to make light of the situation. Remember, you control the situation. Don't let the situation control you.

THE BEGINNING

Normally you would call the last chapter of the book an epilogue, or conclusion, or some kind of summary. But neither of these words would adequately describe the contents of my last departing words. A conclusion or final chapter signifies the end of the something. It means that it has been concluded or finished. There is nothing more to be said or done. This is not the case when it comes to improving your life and benefiting others.

This is not the end of your work to be a better communicator. This is just the beginning. My book is designed to get your feet firmly on the road to being a more persuasive speaker. It is designed to help you overcome your fears and take you to a new level of communication. I wrote this book to put the power of your life's destiny into the hands of the most capable person who can handle it, that's you. Being able to articulate your ideas and present them to the world is one of the most powerful skills that you can learn. It is a skill that will be with you for the rest of your life.

They can take away your job, your possessions and maybe even your friends. But they can't take away what is in your mind. And now this book is a part of you forever. I have armed you with a process, tools, and skills that can never be taken away. They are yours forever. But even a person armed with all this can fail if they are not used correctly. You must implement these skills, continually practice, and seek feedback for the greatest benefits to you and to those with whom you are trying to reach with your message.

This is not the end, it is the beginning. You now have the knowledge that can be turned into power. I encourage you to read this book over and over again until these practices become a part of you.

RESOURCES

Great Web Sites to explore:

Interested in going pro or just want to learn the secrets of the pros?
www.nsaspeaker.org

Join a volunteer speaking organization like Toastmasters.
www.toastmasters.org

Need professional coaching or training?
www.speakingsmart.com

Books for Your Career:

To understand the importance of being a leader and communicator:

Martin Luther King, Jr. on Leadership	Donald T. Phillips
Lincoln on Leadership	Donald T. Phillips
Victory Secrets of Attila the Hun	Wess Roberts, Ph.D
Networlding	Mellisa Giovagnoli
	Jocelyn Carter-Miller

The 7 Habits of Highly Effective People	Stephen R. Covey

Here are some books to help get you motivated and empowered:

The Procrastinators Handbook	Rita Emmett
First Things First	Stephen Covey
The Alladin Factor (tape) (A must listen to)	Jack Canfield & Mark Victor Hansen

What to do to change gears in your career (the best):

What Color is Your Parachute	Richard Nelson Bolles

The importance of making the connection with your listener:

Relationship Marketing	Regis Mckena
Guerilla Marketing	Jay Conrad Levinson
The One to One Future	Don Peppers & Martha Roberts Ph.D
The Psychology of Persuasion	Robert B. Cialdini, Ph.D
Soft Sell	Tim Conner

How to communicate one on one:

Difficult Conversations	Douglas Stone, Bruce Patton Sheila Heen
The Power of Positive Confrontation	Barbara Pachter
Skill with People (Hard to get;. contact me if you can't find it)	Les Giblin

Heavy duty reading and exercise:

Inspire Any Audience (Long on details, good reference)	Tony Jeary

Speaking Smart Training

Reginal Smith has trained community volunteers, managers, and directors in effective communication and leadership skills. Speaking Smart designs and develops training programs for businesses. The courses are customized to the needs of the organization. Reginal is familiar with the corporate environment and the challenges employees are facing the in the work place.

Speaking Smart training does not consist of useless lectures and textbooks. The sessions are interactive, informative and constructed to give attendees a feeling of accomplishment. Each course is packaged with tips and techniques which can be applied immediately in the real world.

Speaking Smart courses are designed with the busy professional in mind. Classes are kept small so as to give each student individual attention and instruction. Courses are also offered via online seminars.

Speaking Smart can custom design courses to meet the specific needs of your business. The Speaking Smart methods are designed to have maximum impact in the organization with a minimum investment of time in training.

Training Courses

- Public Speaking Seminars– OffSite/Onsite training in presentation skills
- Empowerment Networking– Building connections for knowledge sharing.
- Meeting Effectiveness– Increase productivity, and decrease meeting time.
- Team Building– Building High Performance Teams
- Conflict Management– Effectively handling interpersonal issues in the work place
- Mentoring– Creating an effective mentoring program
- Coaching– Getting the best out of your employees
- Transformational Change– Managing and embracing change
- Project Management- Effective techniques for managing projects

For additional information on training, contact Reginal Smith
Email: rsmithspeakingsmart@com
Website: www.speakingsmart.com
phone: 888 SPEAKS4

Attend the
Speaking Secrets of the Bored Room
Boot Camp

To be an effective leader in your organization, you must have the ability to speak. Speaking to an audience is the most effective communication tool available to a leader. Even for those not seeking to be leaders, they should know how to make an effective presentation, because we are all at some level looking to persuade and influence people.

Speaking Smart teaches the world's only public speaking boot camp. The boot camp is an intensive speaking course. The course concentrates on developing effective presenters with interactive and practice speech sessions. All the fundamentals of making effective presentations are taught. A follow up session with a training coach is included.

Key Benefits
- Learn to Persuade and Influence through speaking
- Effective techniques to gain credibility, trust, rapport with the audience
- Use Visual Aids in Speaking to an Audience
- How to Craft Your message in 30 seconds

For Additional Information Contact:
rsmith@speakingsmart.com
www. Speakingsmart.com
888 SPEAKS4

Special bonus: Free teleseminar for *Speaking Secrets for the Bored Room*. Check www.speakingsmart.com

About the Author

Reginal Smith is a dynamic award winning speaker and writer. He speaks on subjects dealing with workplace empowerment and leadership development. Reginal believes that all training should have a measurable impact in the workplace. Training should make the workplace an environment for innovation and creativity. He spent 8 years in the Marines and 18 years working in corporate America. Reginal is originally from Atlanta, GA., but currently makes his home in Herndon, VA. He is a member of the National Speakers Association and the American Society for Training and Development. Reginal is the chairman of Speaking Kids, a nonprofit organization dedicated to teaching public speaking skills to grade school children. Reginal was recently honored with the D.C. School Volunteer of the Year award and the Freddie Mac Foundation Volunteer Family of the Year award for creating a speaking program for elementary school children in the District of Columbia. The program promotes public speaking and leadership.

In the last five years Reginal has conducted leadership development training for effective communications. He received numerous awards for his initiative and creativity with several high profile corporate rollouts. He has trained managers, directors, and technology professionals in effective presentation skills. In 2003 he received the Premier Achievement Award for excellence in teaching. Reginal Smith is a polished professional speaker, writer, and trainer. If you like to have Reginal speak at your next event you can reach him at the following:

Email: rsmithspeakingsmart.com
Phone: 888 SPEAKS4
Website: www.speakingsmart.com

Index

Next Step

In 1989, the Berlin wall fell. The fall of the Berlin wall signaled the collapsing of an old system. In its wake there is freedom and prosperity, and a new release of energy and intellectual capital. The unleashing of the genie has also brought a whirlwind of confusion and chaos. When an old system crumbles, people scramble to look for order and stability. In the midst of the broken rumble are the bright shining gems of opportunity.

We have entered such a period in the business world. The walls of the authoritative driven business model are collapsing. These decrepit infrastructures are struggling to find relevance in a world where the rules of engagement are changing every minute. Among the debris are golden gems of opportunities for you.

Why are we discussing this in a book dedicated to teaching you how to speak? What is the relationship? This book is devoted to making you a leader in your organization. Your organization is in desperate need of your leadership. We can no longer depend upon leadership from the traditional structures which served us well in the last century.

In a rapid changing marketplace, the old leadership paradigm is inadequate for the task. The old style chain of command structure is crumbling and heading for a complete breakdown. It is impossible for those in the top echelons to exercise decision-making and implementation strategies in a timely manner. By the time the problem or issue has filtered up through the ranks, it may have become old news.

New leadership has to come from below, not from the top. It has to come from the trenches where the actual fighting is being done. Here on the frontlines of the business, decisions can be made with efficiency and speed. That leadership has to come from you. You will be the next leader.

When chaos abounds, people need new direction. The old sources are out of touch and lost in a world that is unrecognizable to them. Only you can provide the needed leadership and direction. You have the ideas. They are bottled up inside of you. Now it's time take control as a leader.

How do you get control? Ha! You already have it. You just don't know it. You have expertise and the talent. The only problem is that the world is not aware of what you have to offer. Your voice needs to be heard. I wrote this book to make your voice heard.

I want you to go back to your old jobs with a new attitude. I want you to become a dreamer again. You remember how you used to dream of what your life was going to be like when you grew up. Well, you have not grown up yet. I want you to think of all the possibilities for change in your organization and in yourself. Don't shackle yourself with any limitations, don't prejudge any idea. The sky's the limit. I want you to write out your ideas. Then think about how you are going to use your new voice to espouse your ideas.

Karl Marx spoke of a day when workers would be owners. Today's worker is on the verge of a revolution. Thanks, to our technology the embers of our dissatisfaction with the present unequal system will soon fan into flames of a revolution. Not a revolution requiring the expenditure of blood and flesh. But a revolution of intellectual warfare.

To start the revolution right, you need a theme. Every great revolution has one you know. So I have labeled this, EmpowerU. And the U stands for all of us. When one person is empowered, we all benefit. So here's our manifesto:

All power belongs in the hands of those best able to shape it and use it to the betterment of others. We empower ourselves so as to uplift, encourage, and empower others. We will speak out with confidence. Our ideas and dreams will propel the wings of innovation and imagination. We seek to become the New Leader.

This book is the first in a series of books dealing with empowerment. Each book is designed to give you the power to change your destiny. My ultimate desire is to make you a success.

But what is success? Is it money, fame, power, or glory? If this is your measuring rod for success, your measuring rod is much too short. You are robbing yourself of true success. We must invent a new measuring rod, one that is on the scale of infinity. New Leadership success cannot be measured my mere materialism or the fading illusion of fame or glory. Your success will manifest itself by empowering yourself so that you can empower others.

The entire world is now your stage. And you are the director. You can choose the scripts; the storyline and the characters. Stop having others write the script for you. Now it's your time to kick others out of the director's chair and take control. It's scary when it all lies upon your shoulders. But that's where the real adventure and excitement comes from. Not from the outside, but from the inside. What kind of ending have you envisioned for yourself? Where do you see yourself? How will you spell success? The storyline is yet to be written, and it is time for you to write it out and move forward.

This is not the end, I want you to subscribe to my free electronic newsletter (subscribe at www.speakingsmart.com); Speaking Smart. Every month we discuss techniques and tips that can empower you.